Acknowledgement

I am constantly amazed by the unshakeable support system I have developed over the last decade of my life, and I am deeply grateful to the following people:

To my mother, without whom my entire career would not be possible. The path of my life continues to surprise and delight me every day and no one has been more integral in that than you. Thank you for never once making me wonder if you were proud of me.

To both my fathers, for loving and supporting me as strongly as they possibly could in their very different ways.

To Susan, whose support and enthusiasm for this project from the very first moment was what got me excited about writing this year.

To Jeff, who is responsible for showing me how to fall in love with this city, and to Michelle who continues to help me eat my way across it. If I could acknowledge you two with a corgi, I promise I would.

To Patrick, whose constant support for me and whatever new scheme I've dreamed up that day never fails. You kept me going this year when I wasn't sure how to and I'll never be able to thank you properly. To Akima for your wisdom and insight - I am blown away by your energy to help the people you love and grateful that I get to be a part of it. To Denman, the undisputed king of puns - your thoughtful approach to everything you do is overwhelming and I love it.

To Jesse for somehow always knowing the right thing to share to inspire me and to Elianna for far too many dinnertime giggles - the way you two have forged your own path blows me away. To Jaleen for being my constant parallel - I'll never understand it, but I am so grateful for it. To Justin, whose love and support is always just a few feet away.

To Justin, Andrew N., Katie K., Harley, Laurence, Drue, Paul, Diane, Kyle, Michelle L., Tom, Carla, Amy B., Tom, and David. Thank you for your friendship, your support, and your inspiration over the last few years.

To John, Cathy, Ian, Matt, Andrew, Kurt, Ben, and all the members of DD08 - thank you for letting me learn from you.

To Nathan, Lars, both Seans and Kathleen – thank you for still being so very present in my life after all these years.

To my many brilliant co-workers over the years, who are responsible for everything I know. Thank you for every time you let me look over your shoulder or schemed up a new technique with me. Matt and Sean, you have my sincere appreciation for your technical contributions.

To Dan Weaver, who believed in a 21-year-old me and pushed me into a career I didn't even know I wanted. Thank you for never making me feel stupid, and for taking the time to answer my never-ending stream of questions.

And finally, a special thank you to Harry, my right hand and favorite partner in crime. Thank you for being my daily sounding board and most significant inspiration. The world has simply never felt more possible than it does with you.

About the Reviewers

Matt Grigoryan garnered a fine-tuned creative skill set of over a decade that includes art direction, motion graphics, team management, training, leadership building, graphic design, animation, and traditional layout. He's fluent in Adobe Creative Suite with strong focus on After Effects, Cinema4D, familiar with Maya Suite, and Autodesk Flint/Flame systems.

Matt has worked the gamut—from feature films to broadcast to software development, constantly refining and expanding his creative skill set. His latest adventure of overseeing all motion design at Xbox/Microsoft office in Mountain View has been an exciting one. Previous employers, both staff and freelance include: Autodesk, Banana Republic, Eveo, Genentech, Impact Media Group, Old Navy, PayPal, Microsoft, Safeway, Seagate, and UrsaMinor.

I'd like to thank Jen for trusting me enough and allowing my two cents being included in her fantastic book. I'm proud of her and glad she's in my life, both professionally and personally. As for me, I'd like to thank everyone who's been actively encouraging my development as an artist and a contributor in today's field of graphics. Starting with my parents for accepting my decision to pursue two art degrees, colleagues for providing much needed perspective when needed, and those close to me for being a never-ending fountain of support.

Jonathan Richter lives in the USA and is the founder of Supermassive Studios, an award-winning motion design/3D animation, and video boutique. With an extensive and varied background ranging from music composition to photography, Jonathan has created a company that leverages technology to tell captivating stories. With Cinema 4D, he enjoys pushing the boundaries of what it is capable of. His passion projects include short films and visual effects. In 2011, his short film *The Box* went on to be accepted into several major film festivals. The Supermassive Studios website can be found at the following URL: http://www.SupermassiveStudios.com

Sean Siegler is a Motion Graphics Artist and live Visual Performer based out of San Francisco.

Originally from the Midwest, he ventured to New York to pursue a degree in Film and Video from Pratt Institute.

Since then he has spent many years creating original content and performing live as a VJ across the country. This lead to a discovery of the art of motion graphics and a love affair with Adobe After Effects. 3D was added to his arsenal after it became apparent that Cinema 4D was a different beast and made creation, exploration, and modeling in the 3D space a much more intuitive and creative process than other software packages.

At present he lives in a warehouse in the Dogpatch neighborhood of San Francisco, with his cat Helmet and his darling fiancée Carlyn.

www.PacktPub.com

Support files, eBooks, discount offers and more

You might want to visit www.PacktPub.com for support files and downloads related to your book.

Did you know that Packt offers eBook versions of every book published, with PDF and ePub files available? You can upgrade to the eBook version at www.PacktPub.com and as a print book customer, you are entitled to a discount on the eBook copy. Get in touch with us at service@packtpub.com for more details.

At www.PacktPub.com, you can also read a collection of free technical articles, sign up for a range of free newsletters and receive exclusive discounts and offers on Packt books and eBooks.

http://PacktLib.PacktPub.com

Do you need instant solutions to your IT questions? PacktLib is Packt's online digital book library. Here, you can access, read and search across Packt's entire library of books.

Why Subscribe?

- ◆ Fully searchable across every book published by Packt
- ◆ Copy and paste, print and bookmark content
- ◆ On demand and accessible via web browser

Free Access for Packt account holders

If you have an account with Packt at www.PacktPub.com, you can use this to access PacktLib today and view nine entirely free books. Simply use your login credentials for immediate access.

Table of Contents

Preface

With Cinema 4D, you can quickly and easily bring your visions to life. This beginner's guide will walk you through creating and animating a 3D scene, with tips and techniques for everything from photorealistic rendering to motion graphics.

What this book covers

Chapter 1, Getting to Know Cinema 4D, provides an introduction to 3D space and how to navigate the Cinema 4D interface.

Chapter 2, Modeling Part 1: Edges, Faces, and Points, provides a foundation in polygonal modeling.

Chapter 3, Modeling Part 2: Splines, NURBS, Deformers, and Boole, takes modeling to a new direction by using parametric objects.

Chapter 4, Materials and Shaders, will bring character to your models by adding surface properties.

Chapter 5, Lighting and Rendering, will introduce lighting to add additional realism and dimension to your objects, as well as explore global visual settings.

Chapter 6, Animation, provides an overview of the linear animation process as we animate a camera and lighting in our 3D environment.

Chapter 7, MoGraph, provides a brief overview of many common MoGraph objects such as cloner and tracer, as well as how to work with Cinema 4D's built-in Dynamics system.

Chapter 8, XPresso, provides an introduction to node-based programming showing the usage of Math to connect properties of objects to one another.

Chapter 9, An Overview of Additional Tools, shows how to use Hair, Sketch and Toon, and Cloth.

Chapter 10, *Optimizing Your Workflow*, brings everything we've learned together through exporting multipass renders and spatial data as we composite our final animation in Adobe After Effects.

Appendix: *Pop Quiz Answers*, contains answers to the Pop Quiz sections at the end of *Chapter 2* and *Chapter 5*.

What you need for this book

A basic understanding of computer graphics and linear animation will be helpful, but not necessary. The book provides a step-by-step introduction to working in 3D space as well as working on a timeline. Cinema 4D is our primary tool, but we will also briefly use Adobe Illustrator for drawing Bezier splines and Adobe After Effects for post-production compositing.

Who this book is for

This book is for designers and artists with a basic proficiency in animation or computer graphics, as well as professionals with an understanding of 3D animation in another software package.

Conventions

In this book, you will find several headings appearing frequently.

To give clear instructions of how to complete a procedure or task, we use:

Time for action – heading

1. Action 1
2. Action 2
3. Action 3

Instructions often need some extra explanation so that they make sense, so they are followed with:

What just happened?

This heading explains the working of tasks or instructions that you have just completed.

You will also find some other learning aids in the book, including:

Pop quiz – heading

These are short multiple-choice questions intended to help you test your own understanding.

Have a go hero – heading

These are practical challenges and give you ideas for experimenting with what you have learned.

You will also find a number of styles of text that distinguish between different kinds of information. Here are some examples of these styles, and an explanation of their meaning.

Code words in text are shown as follows: "You may notice that we used the Unix command rm to remove the Drush directory rather than the DOS del command."

A block of code is set as follows:

```
# * Fine Tuning
#
key_buffer = 16M
key_buffer_size = 32M
max_allowed_packet = 16M
thread_stack = 512K
thread_cache_size = 8
max_connections = 300
```

When we wish to draw your attention to a particular part of a code block, the relevant lines or items are set in bold:

```
# * Fine Tuning
#
key_buffer = 16M
key_buffer_size = 32M
max_allowed_packet = 16M
thread_stack = 512K
thread_cache_size = 8
max_connections = 300
```

Any command-line input or output is written as follows:

```
cd /ProgramData/Propeople

rm -r Drush

git clone --branch master http://git.drupal.org/project/drush.git
```

New terms and **important words** are shown in bold. Words that you see on the screen, in menus or dialog boxes for example, appear in the text like this: "On the **Select Destination Location** screen, click on **Next** to accept the default destination.".

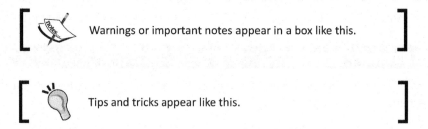

Warnings or important notes appear in a box like this.

Tips and tricks appear like this.

Reader feedback

Feedback from our readers is always welcome. Let us know what you think about this book—what you liked or may have disliked. Reader feedback is important for us to develop titles that you really get the most out of.

To send us general feedback, simply send an e-mail to feedback@packtpub.com, and mention the book title through the subject of your message.

If there is a topic that you have expertise in and you are interested in either writing or contributing to a book, see our author guide on www.packtpub.com/authors.

Customer support

Now that you are the proud owner of a Packt book, we have a number of things to help you to get the most from your purchase.

Downloading the color images of this book

We also provide you a PDF file that has color images of the screenshots/diagrams used in this book. The color images will help you better understand the changes in the output. You can download this file from http://www.packtpub.com/sites/default/files/downloads/2144OT_Cinema_4D_Beginners_Guide.pdf

Errata

Although we have taken every care to ensure the accuracy of our content, mistakes do happen. If you find a mistake in one of our books—maybe a mistake in the text or the code—we would be grateful if you would report this to us. By doing so, you can save other readers from frustration and help us improve subsequent versions of this book. If you find any errata, please report them by visiting http://www.packtpub.com/support, selecting your book, clicking on the **errata submission form** link, and entering the details of your errata. Once your errata are verified, your submission will be accepted and the errata will be uploaded to our website, or added to any list of existing errata, under the Errata section of that title.

Piracy

Piracy of copyright material on the Internet is an ongoing problem across all media. At Packt, we take the protection of our copyright and licenses very seriously. If you come across any illegal copies of our works, in any form, on the Internet, please provide us with the location address or website name immediately so that we can pursue a remedy.

Please contact us at copyright@packtpub.com with a link to the suspected pirated material.

We appreciate your help in protecting our authors, and our ability to bring you valuable content.

Questions

You can contact us at questions@packtpub.com if you are having a problem with any aspect of the book, and we will do our best to address it.

Getting to Know Cinema 4D

Cinema 4D is a popular tool for hobbyists, students, and professionals, due to its user-friendly interface and ease of integration into additional pieces of software. Users of other instances of design software such as Adobe Photoshop or Adobe Illustrator will notice strong similarities in the default layout. This chapter will serve as an introduction to Cinema's interface so that the tools we refer to later on will be easier to find.

In this chapter we will cover the following topics:

◆ Understanding how 3D space is emulated on a 2D screen

◆ Exploring Cinema's main interface elements

◆ Exploring the viewport and our display options

◆ Creating basic primitives and discussing the difference between parametric and polygonal objects

◆ Introducing our project for this book—an animated flythrough of an office

Before we begin

In order to install Cinema, you'll need a computer that fits the following requirements:

◆ Windows XP, Vista, or 7 running on an Intel or AMD CPU with SSE2-Support

◆ Mac OS X 10.5.8 or higher running on an Intel-based Mac

◆ 1024 MB of free RAM

◆ DVD ROM drive

◆ Standard DVD installation can take up to 7 GB of disk space

Additional information can be found on MAXON's website at the following link:

◆ `http://www.maxon.net/products/general-information/general-information/system-requirements.html`

There are four different packages of Cinema available for purchase, as follows:

◆ Prime

◆ Broadcast

◆ Visualize

◆ Studio

Prime is MAXON's basic offering, which offers a toolset for anyone looking for basic 3D animation functionality. This version should be sufficient for students and will contain most of the features mentioned in this book (MoGraph, which will be discussed in *Chapter 7, MoGraph*, is available in Broadcast and Studio only). Broadcast targets motion graphics professionals, while Visualize is directed at architects and designers. Studio contains all of the features from the other three versions. The different versions are designed to offer necessary functionality at a lower cost for specific industries. A full product comparison can be found on MAXON's website (`http://www.maxon.net/products/general-information/general-information/product-comparison.html`).

MAXON has always done an excellent job of ensuring that its software supports a wide range of computers dating back multiple years. R12 was the first version that did not support PPC Macintosh computers, almost five years after Intel-based Macs became standard and well after most major animation and design software applications had discontinued support. While Cinema can be installed on many older machines, 3D software is notorious for being a processor hog. A multiprocessor machine with ample RAM is recommended, and render speeds will be much improved on more powerful machines.

It isn't a requirement for installation, but a standard three-button mouse is highly recommended. Many shortcuts can be accessed by left-, right-, and center-clicking with a mouse. It's not impossible to use Cinema without one, but you'll find it much easier.

A note for users of previous versions is that R13 represents a major shift in Cinema's core architecture. While many of the principles in this book will apply to R11.5 and R12, we will be focusing specifically on R13. If you are unable to find a tool in the location specified here, start by searching in the software's **Help** section. If you are still unable to find it, it may be a feature specific to R13. A full list of new features can be found on MAXON's website at: `http://www.maxon.net/products/general-information/general-information/all-new-r13-features.html`.

Understanding 3D space

Up until now, it's very likely that all of the work you've ever done on a computer has been in 2D space. Text documents, e-mails, videos are all there on a flat surface. When we draw a box, we click and hold on the screen, draw the box to the dimensions we need, and release. We're left with a rectangle—a shape with an X and Y dimension.

Pick up a nearby object and examine it. If you took a photo of it and put it on your computer, it might be 500 x 300, but you'd only be seeing part of the object; an image, rather than an object. Who knows what might be on the bottom or the back; you've only got part of the information! By holding it in your hand, you can turn it around, see where it bulges out and where it contracts, where its edges are sharp, and where they gently curve.

If you've ever had to create a perspective drawing, you know that it takes a little practice to wrap your mind around how objects and environments look from a certain angle. Imagine a photo of a long road stretching ahead of you—the road closest to you appears much wider than the road far off in the distance, but we know that the road is actually of a consistent width and our eye, or the camera's eye in this case, is forcing a certain perspective. So if we sit down with a pencil and paper, or open Photoshop to try and create a rendering of what we see, we have to figure out how to visually force that perspective in our composition as well.

In 3D software, you're creating the object in the same way you'd create it in real life. A cube is made up of six perfectly equal squares that come together at 90 degree angles. The perspective you see in 3D renderings is entirely dependent on the camera angle, which means once we've created an object, we can create a rendering from infinite angles with little additional effort, as shown in the following screenshot:

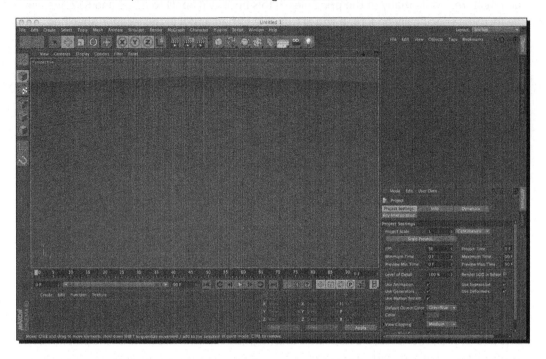

As we move on to exploring Cinema's interface, it's important to establish our coordinate system – how 3D space and direction are represented on our 2D screen. When we modify an object, we'll often have to specify if we're modifying it in one, two, or three dimensions, as well as which dimensions we're choosing to modify. When you open Cinema 4D, you'll see a perspective grid. The center point represents (0,0,0). The red arrow represents the X axis, the blue arrow represents the Z axis, and the upward dimension (which will be colored green when we begin creating objects) is the Y axis.

The xyz coordinate system is what we'll use for both position and scale, but rotation is represented by the **Heading, Pitch, Bank (HPB)** coordinate system. H rotates on the x-z plane, P rotates on the y-z plane, and B rotates on the x-y plane. Let's begin exploring the menus so all of those letters make a little more sense!

Main Menu and Command Palettes

The **Main Menu** is located at the top of the screen. Commands in Cinema can often be accessed in a variety of ways—it's common to have a keyboard shortcut, a location in a drop-down menu, and an icon to accomplish the same task. As you progress through this book, you'll most certainly develop your own preferred method. When we introduce a new tool, we'll explore multiple options to access it, but will default to the Command Palette when we call on that tool again. For example, we can create a cube by navigating to **Create | Objects | Cube**, but we can also click on the cube icon in our Command Palette. Certain functions can only be accessed via the Main Menu, so we'll refer this area for less common commands. The following is a screenshot of the Main Menu:

The row of icons located underneath the Main Menu, as well as the icons on the left-hand side of the screen, represent Cinema's most common functions and are referred to as the **Command Palette**. This is shown in the following screenshot:

These icons are broken into Command Groups, which represent related commands. These Command Groups are as follows:

- Undo/Redo
- Select/Move/Scale/Rotate
- Axis selection
- Render controls
- Object creation

To access an expanded menu, click and hold on any icon with a black arrow on the bottom-right corner. Clicking and holding on the Primitives icon (cube) gives you access to Cinema's built-in objects. Releasing the mouse on one of these objects will add it to your scene; releasing the mouse without selecting an object will leave the submenu expanded and allow you to click again to select an object, as shown in the following screenshot:

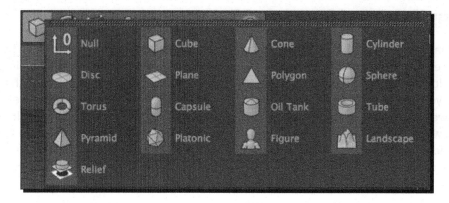

Let's select the **Cube** icon to place a cube in our scene. When you create a cube, you'll notice three arrows appear. Our **Move** tool is selected as the default option, as shown in the following screenshot:

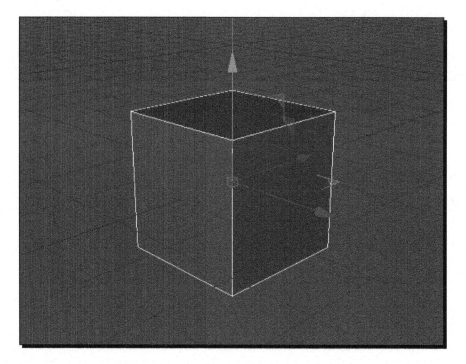

If you click-and-drag anywhere on the window, it will move your cube in the direction of your mouse in all three directions. This is because we haven't locked ourselves into an axis yet. Notice in the top bar that the X, Y, and Z icons are all selected. Deselect the X axis, then click-and-drag; the cube now only moves in two directions. If you want your cube to move only in one direction, you can either deselect two of the three icons, or simply select the specific arrow on your cube and drag it to the desired position, locking yourself in to the selected axis. You'll also notice red, blue, and green triangles just to the outside of our cube—these represent axis bands, which confine movement to just two axes:

The icons on the left-hand side of the screen represent methods of interacting with objects. Depending on the task at hand, all these steps may not be necessary, but the basic order of operations is to select an icon on the left (allowing you to control an entire object, point, edge, or face), then select a command from the top (move, scale, rotate) and then select an axis (X, Y, Z). So if we want to move an object on the Y axis, we'd select the object icon, then the move icon, and deselect the X and Z axes.

Viewport

The center section of Cinema's interface is called the Viewport. This is where you'll be able to view all the objects in your scene. Let's create a cube so that we have an object to orient ourselves.

At the top-left corner of the **Viewport**, you'll see six menu options: **View**, **Cameras**, **Display**, **Options**, **Filter** and **Panel**. If you click and hold on the small 4x4 grid to the left of **View**, you'll notice the icon changes to blue. If you move the window around, you'll notice a bar aligning on the edges of neighboring windows. This allows you to customize your layout by moving individual panels anywhere you choose in order to tailor your software to your workflow. Additional pre-defined layouts can be found in the **Layout** drop-down menu at the top-right corner of your screen. For consistency, we'll use the **Standard** layout for this book.

The viewport allows you to view and move around the objects in your scene. At the top right of the viewport, you'll see four icons, which represent common commands for the viewport. This is shown in the following screenshot:

Clicking and holding on the first three icons allows you to pan, zoom, and rotate the viewport. These camera adjustments can also be accessed via your keyboard by holding down *1* (Pan), *2* (Zoom), or *3* (Rotate) as you click-and-drag with the mouse. If holding down *2* or *3* to zoom or rotate, you'll notice that the previous position of the mouse cursor is replaced with a crosshair. This represents the anchor point for your camera movement. If we hover over the top-right corner of our cube, press *2* on the keyboard and move the mouse, we'll zoom in to that corner. If the mouse is not hovering over an object, the anchor point defaults to our background, enabling faster, world-oriented camera movement. You can also navigate using the left, middle, and right mouse buttons while holding down the *Alt* (Windows) or *Option* (Mac) key.

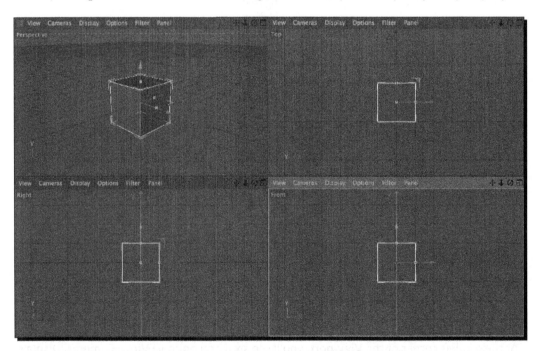

Clicking on the fourth icon shows you additional views—**Top**, **Right**, and **Front**, as shown in the preceding screenshot. These are orthographic cameras and do not show perspective. When working in 3D, it's important to remember that what looks correct in one viewport may not be accurate in another.

If you're exclusively working in a perspective camera, you may arrange objects in a way that looks correct for your current view, but when you move the camera, you'll see that you've accidentally intersected objects or moved them in an incorrect direction. Working with multiple angles open at once is an easy way to ensure that you're making the intended adjustments to your model. In our new four-camera view, you'll notice each window has its own individual menu bar. Clicking the fourth icon in any of these cameras will expand that view to fill the available viewport area. You can also switch between views by clicking with your center mouse button. While in single-camera mode, clicking on the center mouse button will expand all four views. To expand an individual view from four-camera mode, hover your mouse over your chosen view and click on the center mouse button, as shown in the following screenshot:

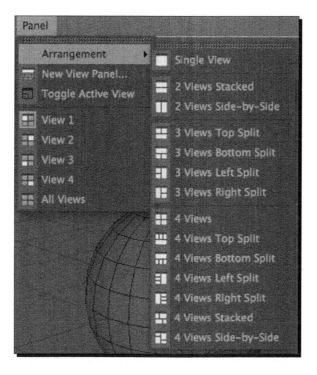

Navigating to **Panel** | **Arrangement** will give you alternatives to the standard four-camera view. If, for example, you're working on detailing just the top of an object, you might not be as interested in the **Right** and **Front** views, and want to see the **Perspective** and **Top** views at the same time; you could select **2 Views Stacked** to gain more screen space for each view.

Let's explore additional viewport options. The **Cameras** menu gives you an additional way to view your object through different cameras and brings up more options than the Top/Right/ Front from our four-camera view. While in four-camera mode, if you select an alternate camera from this menu that is changing **Left** to **Bottom**, Cinema will remember your choice when you switch between views.

You can also create a perspective camera by navigating to **Create | Camera | Camera**, or by clicking on the **Camera** icon in the Command Palette. New cameras are created by default from your current view, so it's easiest to begin by establishing a view that's close to your end goal using our pan/zoom/rotate tools before creating a camera. You can create an endless number of cameras in your scene.

The **Display** menu gives you multiple shading options. This will allow you to see your model as a single smooth object, or as a wireframe, or a combination of both. Let's delete our cube and add a sphere instead (**Create | Object | Sphere**). As we switch between display modes, you will want to deselect the sphere in order to see the most accurate representation, as shown in the following screenshot:

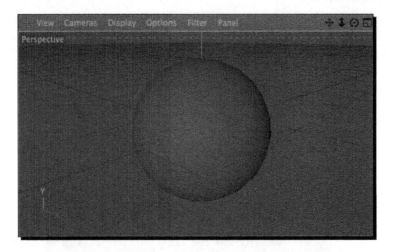

Our default display—**Gouraud**, is set to give us a relatively accurate rendering of the textures and geometry of our object:

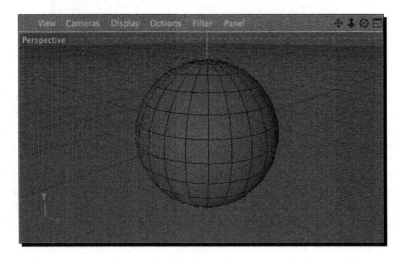

If we change to **Gouraud Shading (Lines)**, you'll see an outline of each of the individual polygons in our object:

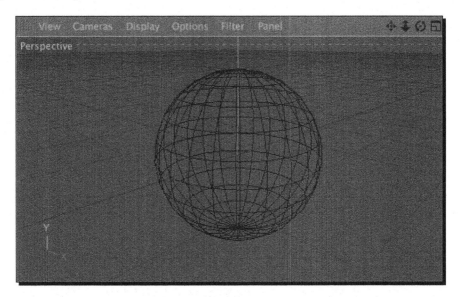

Switching to **Lines** gives us a transparent view of our object only showing edges. Note that these display options have no effect on our final rendered output and changing them will only affect how the object is displayed in the viewport as we work on our scene. If you're working on a more complex file, you may find it helpful to switch to a different mode in order to save processor power.

Render options

The process of turning the on-screen model into an image is called **Rendering**. Rendering takes your scene that looks blocky and segmented during editing and turns it into a smooth, beautiful image. There are many third-party rendering plugins for Cinema, but we'll be using the built-in **Advanced Render** module. The render engine for R13 has been greatly improved by the addition of **Physical Rendering**, which we'll explore in *Chapter 5, Materials and Shaders*. A rendered model looks very different from the on-screen preview, so we'll want to check our progress every once in a while along the way. The following is a screenshot of Render icons in the Command Palette:

The three icons in the center of the Command Palette with the clapboard in the bottom-left are the Render icons. Clicking the icon on the left renders the current **Viewport** window. You can also press *command + R* on a Mac, or *Ctrl + R* on a Windows system. This will not save an external image and only renders a preview in the **Viewport**. Clicking on **Viewport** while it is rendering will cancel the process. The center icon will render to **Picture Viewer** according to the settings you have entered in the window represented by the third icon, **Render Settings**.

Objects and Attributes Manager

When we create a new object, the object name will pop up in a window at the top-right corner of the screen. The following is a screenshot of our Objects Manager:

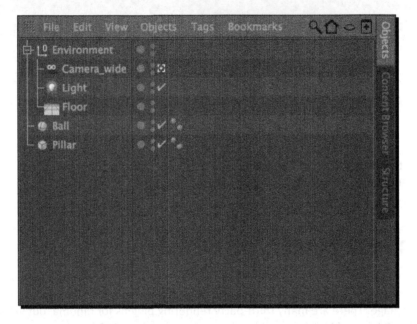

Here, we can rename objects, select groups of objects, create parent-child relationships, and control many other functions. Objects can be selected by clicking on them in the viewport, but often in more complex scenes where one object is obscured from the camera by another, it becomes valuable to be able to select it from a list. It is therefore a good practice to name your objects as you go along, otherwise, we could end up with hundreds of objects named Sphere and Cube and never find anything! At the top-right corner of the window you'll see a magnifying glass icon, which represents the **Search** tool. If your objects are named correctly, it can come in handy as you create more complex scenes. The following is a screenshot of the list of properties of an object (cube) in the Attributes Manager:

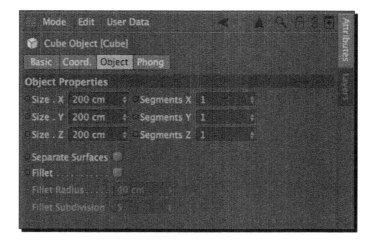

Clicking on an object in the Objects Manager will open a list of properties in the Attributes Manager. The information available in the Attributes Manager varies depending on the type of object. For example, if we create a sphere, we are able to control its radius and segments. For a cube, you can control the size of each of its three dimensions, the number of segments per side, and the radius of the fillet if you've created a cube with rounded edges. As we create additional objects, lights, cameras, and materials, we will regularly access their information in this panel.

Points, edges, faces, and editable objects

Objects in 3D space may look solid, but they are actually hollow—a combination of dots and lines that the software connects to look like real objects. A cardboard box may be hollow, but the cardboard perhaps has thickness of one-eighth of an inch, still giving it some visibility, no matter how thin. A 3D cube, by default, has no thickness whatsoever. The six sides, referred to as **faces** or **polygons** (polys for short), are created by connecting four individual points in space by lines called **edges**. A cube has eight points, and when all of them are connected to one another, these six 2D shapes come together to make a perfectly hollow cube.

It would be easy to manually create a cube (it's only eight points) but certain objects, such as spheres, are much more complicated. Most standard 3D software isn't set to naturally understand curves, so any roundness to an object is created by multiple points in space, connected by straight lines. When enough of those tiny straight lines are put in a row, our eye is tricked into thinking we're looking at a curve. Imagine building a brick archway. If you build your archway using 10 bricks, it will look segmented and choppy. But if you build your archway using 100 bricks, the shape appears much smoother. Objects such as spheres and cylinders can have hundreds of individual polys, so Cinema has built in a number of primitives to save time and effort. They can be found in our **Create** | **Objects** menu that we visited when we began exploring our viewport, or by clicking and holding on the primitives icon.

Primitives and other objects in Cinema have two states: **Parametric** and **Polygonal**. The process of converting an object to a polygon is referred to as "making it editable".

Let's create a cube and examine how we can modify it. When the cube is selected, we can modify it via the Attributes Manager. By default, our cube is 200 cm on all sides. If we want a taller cube, we can enter a new value into the appropriate field in the Attributes Manager. Let's change the Y value to 300.

Another way to modify the object is by using the Scale command. Let's select the **Scale** icon in our Command Manager. We've previously discussed that selecting a single axis locks our transformation to that axis, so let's select just the Z axis and attempt to scale. The cube scales all directions proportionally! This is because our cube is parametric and not polygonal. When primitives are still in their parametric state, many of our controls are disabled. If you select the **Polygon** icon in the left-hand Command Palette and attempt to select just one face of the cube, you'll be unable to click on anything.

With our cube selected, click on the icon at the top-left corner that looks like two spheres with arrows on both sides, as shown in the following screenshot:

This icon converts our object to polygon (this command can also be accessed by pressing *C* on your keyboard). Now, if we select the Scale tool and click-and-drag just on the Y axis, our object will scale in the correct direction.

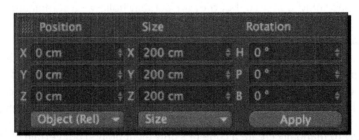

The Coordinate Manager is located to the left-hand side in the Attributes Manager. The Coordinate Manager allows us to enter specific values for position, scale, size, and rotation. You can also use it as a reference when you are scaling objects visually—it will update as you make modifications, so if you know you want to be around a certain value but prefer to eyeball it in your composition, you can spot-check as you go.

Now, we also have access to the **Point**, **Edge**, and **Polygon** modes. Let's select the **Polygon** tool, then move the mouse over our cube. If we click on a highlighted face, note that our axis moves from the center of the cube to the center of the selected face, as follows:

Now if we move the axis, it only affects our selected side. Selecting **Point mode** or **Edge mode** will have a similar effect. However, note that our controls in the Attributes Manager have been replaced with the **Basic Properties** menu instead of our previous options. It is standard practice to leave primitives as parametric options until we specifically need to modify an object. Once the object is converted to polygonal, there is no way to return it to parametric—meaning commands such as filleting (rounding edges), number of faces, and so on will become much more difficult.

Materials Manager

The final piece of the puzzle is the Materials Manager, located to the left of the Attributes Manager, as shown in the following screenshot:

The Materials Manager allows you to see and edit all of the textures you've created in your scene—wood for floors, brick for walls, green leafy textures for outdoor scenes, and so on. Since we have not yet created any materials in our scene, it is currently empty. Double-click in this window (or, in the Materials Manager, select **Create | New Material**) to create a new material. When a material is selected, its properties appear in the Attributes Manager, as follows:

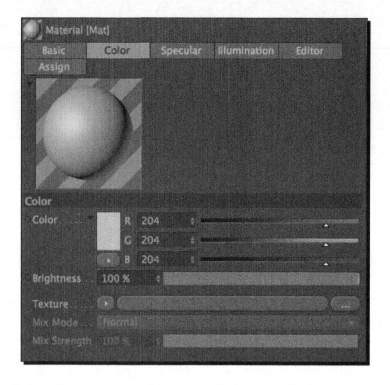

You can also double-click on the material to open it in a new window.

Time for action – customizing the interface

It was mentioned earlier that we'd be staying in Cinema's default layout for the rest of this book for consistency. As you learn how to model, texture, and light your scenes, however, you may find that your workflow is best suited to a different configuration. Thankfully, Cinema's interface is entirely customizable, so you can experiment with what options are most useful to you. Let's dig in and move things around!

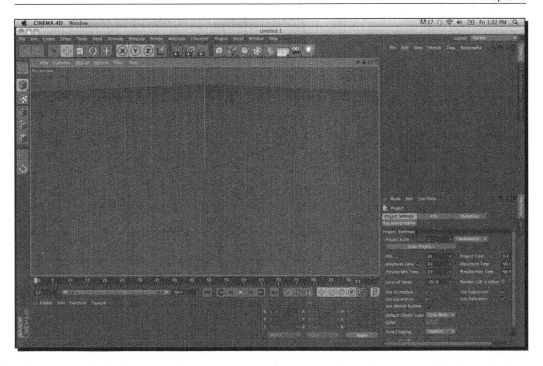

1. Perhaps you're working on a desktop computer or using multiple monitors. Let's imagine you're working on a laptop, or in a situation where screen space is at a premium. The main issue is that you may want a little extra room for your viewport, since that's where most of our work will take place. Let's move and minimize in order to get us some more space.

2. While holding down the *Ctrl* key, click on the gray dots to the left of your timeline (underneath the viewport). Since we're not animating just yet, we can get it out of our way and gain a few extra pixels.

3. Let's take the same action for our animation controls underneath. We can always click on the gray bar to expand our controls later.

4. Early on, particularly when we're focusing on modeling, we may not have a major need for our Materials Manager. It's good to keep this one around, though, since we may want to assign preliminary materials as we go along just so we're ready when it's time to actually texture our objects. Instead of pressing *Ctrl* along with clicking on the corner of the manager, click-and-drag. Release the window above the Attributes Manager. You may also want to change the size of this new window, as all three panels on the right side of the screen will take up equal space by default. Giving more room to the Attributes Manager will still allow us to see a set of materials without compromising too much of our important information below.

5. Repeat the process for the Coordinates Manager. Let's move it on top of the **Materials** window. Again, you may want to adjust the proportions of the windows in order to maximize space where it's needed and take space away from areas we're not accessing as frequently, as shown in the following screenshot:

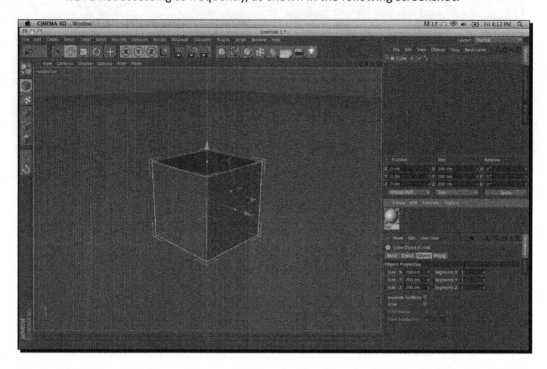

What just happened?

There are a number of reasons to customize your work area. What we've created here is something that functions well on a small screen, is optimized for modeling, but retains all our necessary tools. There are a number of pre-made layouts that are set up for different purposes, which can be accessed via the **Layout** drop-down menu at the top-right corner of your screen. It may be useful to use some of these layouts as a starting point, but once you've found a configuration that works for you, you may want to save it by navigating to **Window | Customization | Save Layout As...**, as Cinema will reset the layout when it closes. You can also save a layout as your default at startup, which is particularly helpful if you're working with multiple monitors.

Hidden menus – M and V

Two additional menus can be accessed by pressing *M* or *V* on the keyboard. The *V* menu is shown in the following screenshot:

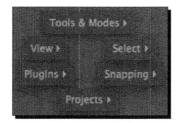

The *V* menu provides a useful shortcut to quickly switch between view and selection options. The *M* menu is shown in the following screenshot:

The *M* menu accesses tools for polygonal modeling. You can select a tool from the list using your mouse, but it also serves as a keyboard shortcut guide, for example, pressing *M* + *K* in order will turn on the Knife tool.

Putting it all together – our project

The best way to learn how to create a 3D animation is to get your hands dirty and make one! In the chapters to come, we'll explore the tools and learn some tricks in Cinema 4D as we create an animated flythrough of an office. We'll learn how to model by exploring various techniques for creating a desk, chairs, and cabinets; we'll create textures to set our pieces apart from one another and add style to our environment; we'll add depth and shine with our lighting, and we'll bring everything to life through animation and rendering.

Summary

At this point, we've started to dig into Cinema and learned a little about all of our main areas. We learned about Viewport and Cameras, which form the main area of our screen where you can move around and modify your models. We also learned about Command Palettes, which provide shortcuts to your main toolset. Finally we saw Objects and Attributes Managers, which help you in selecting and modifying properties of your objects.

Now that we've taken a look at where everything is, let's learn how to use it! Over the next two chapters, we'll learn the ins and outs of modeling as we begin creating our animation. Since we've done some interface exploring in this chapter, there won't be quite as many detailed instructions on where things are located as we go along. If you forget where you left something, you'll always have this chapter as a reference!

2
Modeling Part 1: Edges, Faces, and Points

3D animations are delivered via QuickTime movies, DVDs, or on the Web, but they start as geometric points in space, connected by lines that compose simple 2D shapes. Dimensionality comes from how color and light bounce off of polygons in 3D space. In this introduction to modeling, we'll explore how complex models can be created starting with primitive shapes.

In this chapter we will cover the following topics:

◆ Exploring our Primitives menu

◆ Converting objects from parametric to polygon

◆ Understanding edges, faces, and points and the advantages of each level of control

◆ Exploring Cinema's modeling toolset

Before we begin

The process of building objects in Cinema is often very similar to how you'd build them in real life. Say you want to build a coffee table—you'd go to the hardware store, measure and cut a piece of wood for the top, and measure four equal pieces for the legs. Then you'd attach them all together so they can be moved around as one unit.

Or imagine you're creating a vase—you could take a large lump of clay and carefully sculpt out the shape you desire by hand, or better yet, you could put it on a lathe and ensure that your shape was perfect the entire way around. Both methods are effective, they just yield slightly different results.

As we move forward into modeling, it's going to be easy to get lost in the details, so it's important to routinely take a step back and examine your model from a high-level perspective. Reference images, or better yet, an actual tangible version of what you want to make, will come in handy.

Beginning with primitives

Referring back to our vase analogy, we will spend this chapter and the next focusing on two different methods. This chapter will take a look at the by-hand sculpting method, and we'll dive into the lathe method in *Chapter 3, Modeling Part 1: Splines, NURBS, Deformers, Boole*.

Let's begin by becoming familiar with the different properties of commonly used primitives. This will get us thinking about how we can shape our figurative "lumps of clay" into real, recognizable objects. The following is a screenshot of our Primitives menu:

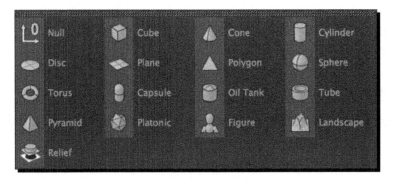

The first thing we'll model for our office will be a desk. Looking at our Primitives menu, a couple of key things will stand out—we'll certainly want to use a cube for our tabletop, and we'll need to create legs by either using additional cubes or cylinders.

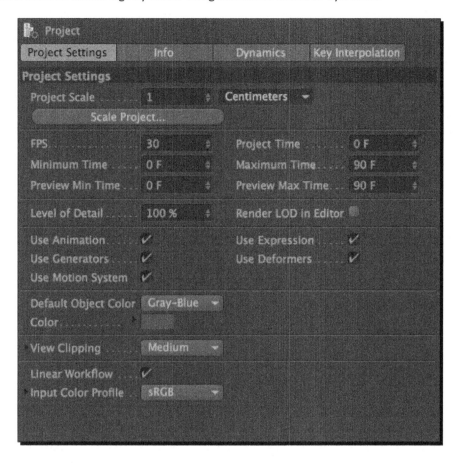

Cinema 4D supports real-world measurements. For the purposes of this book, we'll be using centimeters, but if you feel more comfortable working in a different scale, you can change it at any time. Note that changing the scale will simply convert your measurement, so if you're working in inches and you switch to centimeters, a 200-inch cube will now read as 508 centimeters, rather than just changing the display units and forcing your cube to be 200 centimeters. If you wish to change the scale, open your **Project Settings** tab under the **Project** window at **Edit | Project Settings**. The following is a screenshot of our **Project window**: It's also useful to change the scale depending on the sort of project you're creating. A mobile phone may be easiest to work on in millimeters, while our office is best suited for inches or centimeters; but if we were working on an exterior scene, we might want to choose feet or meters. Since changing the unit does not affect the absolute scale of the file, we can switch back and forth to whatever is most appropriate at the time. If you are working on a project with a team, it's common practice to make sure everyone is working in the same scale to ensure consistency as files are traded back and forth between artists. The following is a screenshot of the **Cube Object** window:

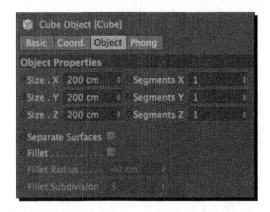

Let's first examine the attributes of a cube. The default size is **200 cm** (or 200*x*, where *x* is your unit size if you're not working in centimeters) on all sides. If your end goal is to just have a simple cube, then the default segment settings (one segment per side) will be sufficient. However, if you're using the cube as a starting point for more complex geometry, you can create additional polygons (referred to as **subdividing**) by changing the **Segments** values. With the cube selected, change the **Segments X** value to 10. You'll notice that our cube is now divided into multiple sections along the X axis. In order to not increase our polygon count (which will increase render time), it's best to keep these segment values as low as possible. If you render the current view, you'll notice the cube looks exactly the same, since we've simply divided the cube and not modified anything else about it. This will not be the case for objects like spheres and other curved objects, as the smoothness of the curve is determined by the number of segments on an object, but we'll cover that later as we explore additional primitives. The number of segments you assign to an object will mostly be important once we convert an object from parametric to polygonal, as discussed in *Chapter 1, Getting to Know Cinema 4D*.

In addition to size and segments, we can also turn on the **Separate Surfaces** and **Fillet** options. **Separate Surfaces** detaches the sides of the cube from one another and is another option that will generally only be useful if we are converting our object to polygon. Turning on **Fillet** will round the edges of our cube and allow us to control the radius and number of subdivisions. A higher subdivision count will result in a smoother curve, but also increase polygon count and should only be set as high as necessary to achieve the look you desire. Changing this value to 1 results in no curve at all, but instead bevels the edges of our cube.

Let's set our cube to 200 cm on all sides with **Fillet Radius** of 5 cm and **Fillet Subdivision** of 1, then render. Our edges look slightly rounded instead of angular, like they appear before rendering. This is due to our **Phong Angle** settings, seen in the following screenshot:

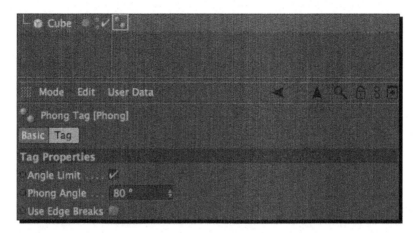

Phong shading is a technique developed for 3D modeling that allows surfaces to appear smoother than their geometry would otherwise force it to appear. This allows you to create spheres that have low-to-mid-range polygon counts that still render as smooth, continuous objects. In the Object Manager, you'll see an icon to the right of our cube that looks like two spheres set diagonally from one another. This area will hold all of our tags as we move forward. Tags are used for many things, including materials, animation, and composition. Select **Phong Tag**. In the Attributes Manager, change the **Phong Angle** value from **80** to **20**, then render. Now our edges are perfectly sharp! The higher the **Phong Angle** value, the smoother the edges of your object will appear.

When you create a cylinder, you'll notice that the options in the Attributes Manager are significantly different and that there are multiple new options at the top of the window, as shown in the following screenshot:

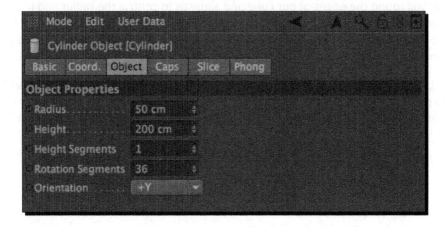

You can adjust the **Radius**, **Height**, **Height Segments**, and **Rotation segments** under the **Object** tab. The **Fillet** option is underneath the **Caps** tab. The **Slice** tab allows you to cut a chunk out of your cylinder.

We'll discuss additional primitives as we continue modeling, but for now, let's get started!

Time for action – creating a desk

Now that we've learned about some of our options for our primitives, let's use them to create a simple desk!

1. Create a cube with dimensions 80 cm x 4 cm x 60 cm. This will be the top of our desk.

2. In the Coordinates Manager, change the Y position to 60 cm. If this moves the cube out of the current viewport, move the viewport until you find it again. You can also hit the *O* key on your keyboard, which will frame the viewport around the currently surrounded object. If no object is selected, there will be no change to the viewport.

3. Create a cylinder with a radius of 2 cm and a height of 59 cm. Move its X position to 35 cm, Y position to 29.5 cm, and Z position to 25 cm.

4. With the cylinder still selected, click and hold on the **Array** icon (the fourth icon in the palette that contains our primitives), then select **Instance**, as shown in the following screenshot. This will create a new object, **Cylinder Instance**. This object is a copy of our cylinder that relies on the original for all of its information. Since they're linked, if we change the original cylinder, the copy will automatically update. Change its X position to 35 cm.

5. Copy and paste **Cylinder Instance**. Change its Z position to 25.

6. Copy and paste the new **Cylinder Instance**. Change its X position to 35.

7. Switch to the **Top** camera. You should see a large rectangle with four circles in each corner. Compare your setup with the following screenshot:

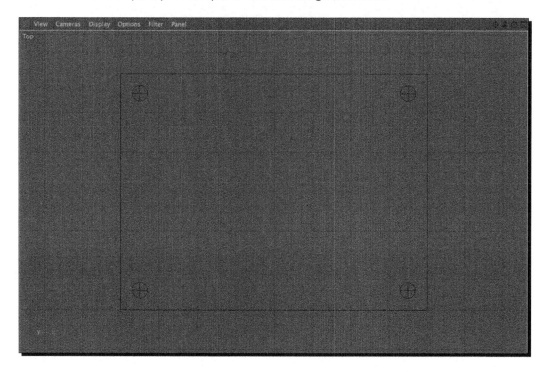

What just happened?

Switch back to the **Perspective** viewport and take a look! You've got something that looks an awful lot like a basic table. We mentioned earlier that when you're building a real table, everything attaches so it can be moved as a single object, though, we don't quite have that just yet. To finish the job, let's make sure all of our objects are correctly named and organized, in case we need to quickly locate them later. You can rename objects in the Objects Manager by double-clicking on their name in the list. Rename each of the table legs to `Leg`, rename our cube to `tabletop`, then click-and-drag each leg on top of the tabletop and release. This will parent (group) each of the legs, so when we want to move them as a group, we can simply select the top and the rest will follow. Click on **Render** to make sure everything's where it should be. Your screenshot should look like the following one:

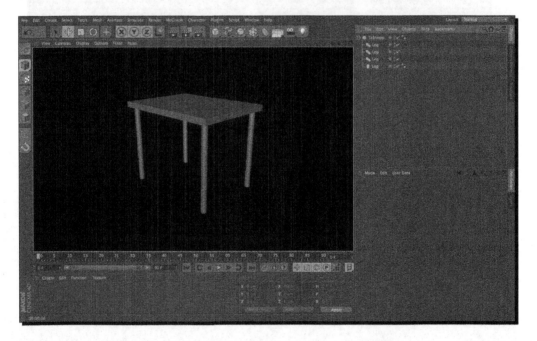

Before we go any further, let's create the basic structure for our room.

Time for action – setting up an environment

We're using real-world dimensions for our objects, but as we create new models, it may help us gain a better sense of scale and proportion if we create an environment for them.

1. First, click on the **Floor** icon (sixth from the left in the palette with the Primitives menu). This will create an infinite plane under our desk.

2. Create a cube with dimensions 600 cm x 300 cm x 20 cm. Change its position to 0, 150, 300. Rename it as `Wall`.

3. With **Wall** selected, create an instance. Change its position to 300, 150, 0. Change the H rotation value to 90.

4. Create a camera by clicking on the Camera icon in the palette to the right of the Render icons. Move it to 415 cm, 165 cm, -415 cm, with an H rotation of 45, and a P and B rotation of 0. In the viewport, navigate to **Camera | Use Camera | Camera**, or click on the icon to the right of the camera object in the **Objects Manager**. We are now looking through a camera at a height of 165 cm—a fairly standard human height. While we model, we will switch in and out of this camera, but we will be able to return at any time to get a sense of scale of our room.

5. Create a second Floor object. Rename it as `Ceiling` and change its Y position to 300 cm.

6. Click on the **Render** button and take a look at what we've set up! Your screenshot should look like the following one:

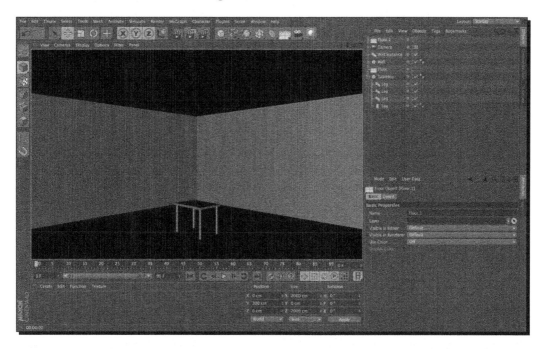

What just happened?

Without relative objects, it's difficult to understand the scale of our model as we create them. If you have a small living room, you probably don't want to put a 72-inch television screen on the wall, right? When you begin creating scenes with a specific end goal, it's important to set up certain constraints and make scale decisions early, otherwise you'll be compelled to constantly scale, move, and resize, taking time away from the fun part, which is making new objects! With the scale of our room decided—300-cm tall, 600 cm on either side—we'll be able to create chairs, tables, lamps, and wall fixtures knowing everything will work together and fit properly.

We're now able to move forward and add additional objects to our office!

Polygon-level control

Now that we're familiar with moving and grouping objects, let's look at how we can turn a simple primitive object into something more complex. Our Polygon controls can be located at either **Mesh | Create Tools...** or by pressing *M* on our keyboard. We'll refer to these tools quite a bit over the next few pages, so take a moment to look at the list and familiarize yourself with the commands.

Now that we've created our environment, our desk looks a little small. Let's create something a little grander, shall we? We'll strive for a modern aesthetic with our room, so we'll start by creating a different, modern desk that will look a little more appropriate in our space.

As we progress, we may decide that something we've made doesn't quite fit, but we don't want to throw it away forever. Look at the tabletop object we created previously. Between the name and the green checkmark, you'll see two dots stacked vertically. Clicking on them once will turn them green, while clicking on them twice turns them red, as shown in the following screenshot:

These dots can be controlled individually, or you can save time by holding down the *Alt* key to change both at once. The top dot represents an object's visibility in the viewport. The bottom dot represents an object's visibility at render time. A green dot means an object is visible, red makes it invisible. So if you want to keep an object around, you can simply turn off its visibility! Be aware if you do this with multiple complex objects, your file size may increase and be more difficult to navigate. Since our desk was so simple, we should have no problems leaving it in the file in case we want to access it later.

Time for action – extruding polygons

In this section, we'll explore how to create a modern, single-piece desk by pushing and pulling, or extruding polygons from a cube. Similar to how we created a desk the first time around, we'll begin by creating a cube for our tabletop, then work on the legs.

1. Let's create a cube. The scale of the room we've created might call for something slightly larger than what we had before, so let's make our cube 150 cm x 8 cm x 90 cm, and change its position to 60 cm.

2. Change the segment values for X and Z to 3. Leave Y at 1.

3. Click on the **Convert** icon at the top-left corner of the screen, or press *C* on your keyboard. This converts our object from parametric to polygon.

4. Click on the **Polygon** icon to activate **Polygon Mode**, then navigate to **Select | Loop Selection** (you can also press *U* + *L* on your keyboard), as shown in the following screenshot:

5. Select the center loop of polygons on the longest side of the desk. The size should currently be 50 cm, since our X value of 150 cm is evenly divided into three sections. Change this value to 130 cm. Your center section will scale, shrinking the outside sections to 10 cm, as follows:

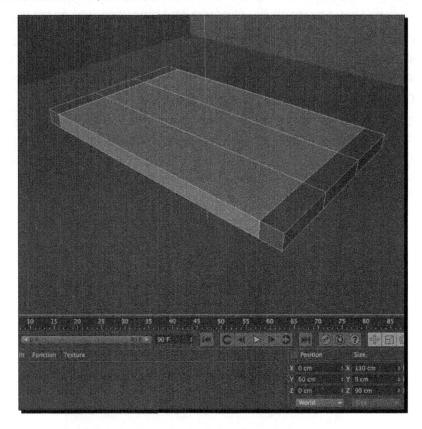

6. Your **Loop Selection** tool may still be selected, but if not, press *U + L* on your keyboard to select it. Then select the center section on the horizontal side. Change the Z value from **30** to **70**. Now we have a 10 cm loop around the outside of our desk.

7. Make sure you are not currently looking through the camera we created previously. The icon to the right of the camera will be white if you are looking through that camera currently, and gray if you are not. Move and rotate the editor camera so you can see the bottom of the desk. If the screen turns gray, there's a chance you've rotated too far and are blocked by the floor.

8. Click on the **Live Selection** icon, and then as you hold down *Shift*, select the outer ring of polygons, except for the center polygon on one of the long sides (you can also press the space bar to toggle between **Live Selection** and the previously used tool), as shown in the following screenshot:

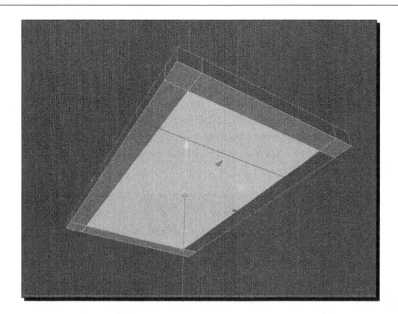

9. With these polygons selected, press *D* on your keyboard. This opens the **Extrude** command. Set the offset to 25 cm, and then click on **Apply**. You can also visually extrude by clicking-and-dragging anywhere in the viewport, as shown in the following screenshot:

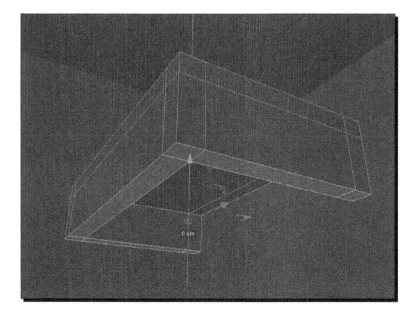

10. Deselect the long center polygon on the remaining continuous side by holding *Ctrl* on your keyboard. The **Extrude** command may still be open; if it isn't, press *D* on your keyboard. The previous value of 25 cm is still shown. Click on **Apply** (if for any reason **Apply** is grayed out, you can also click on **New Transform**).

11. With the bottom polygons still selected, change their Y position value to 3 cm.

12. Select the four corner polygons and press the letter *I* on your keyboard. This activates the **Extrude Inner** command. Change the offset value to 1 cm and click on **Apply**. The bottom polygons should now be inset, as shown in the following screenshot:

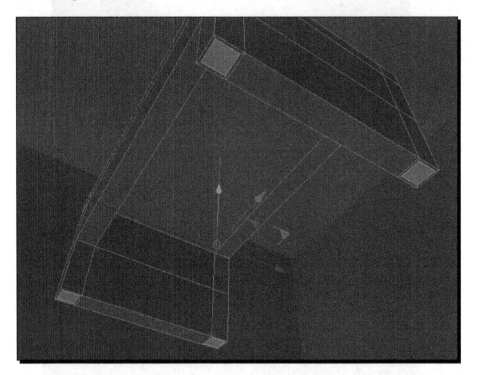

13. With the polygons shown in the previous screenshot still selected, press *D* to open the **Extrude** command. Enter an offset value of 3 cm and click on **Apply**. This will create a new extrusion, as shown in the following screenshot:

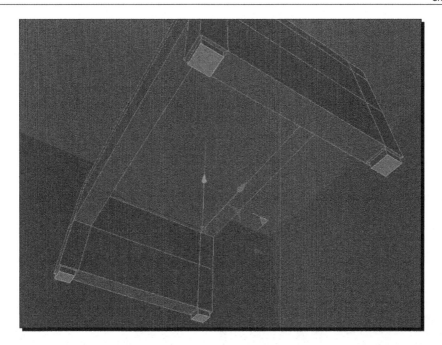

14. Let's look through our camera at what we've created. Click on the icon to the right of our camera. The icon should turn white, indicating that it is being used as our active camera in the viewport. When we render our model, it should appear similar to the following screenshot:

What just happened?

We've created a grander desk that's better suited for our space, is created from fewer polygons, and is visually interesting to boot! Make sure you save. You may want to enable **Auto-Save**, located at **Edit | Preferences | Files**. Larger files will take longer to save, so you may want to change the value of **Every (min)** to **15** or **30 minutes** instead of **5**. To save on hard drive space, you can lower the value of **Limit To (Copies)**.

If you aren't sure about the size of the desk, it's easy to use either the polygon or point tools to change the size. Select the **Point Mode** icon, then click and hold on the **Live Selection** icon to expand the menu, then select **Rectangular Selection**. In the options menu in the **Attributes Manager**, make sure **Only Select Visible Elements** is deselected.

Then, click on the viewport with your middle mouse button to expand into the four-camera mode. In one of the side views, click-and-drag a rectangle across the second row of points from the top. Then, with the Move axis activated, drag up and down in the Y direction until you have a proportion you're happy with, as shown in the following screenshot:

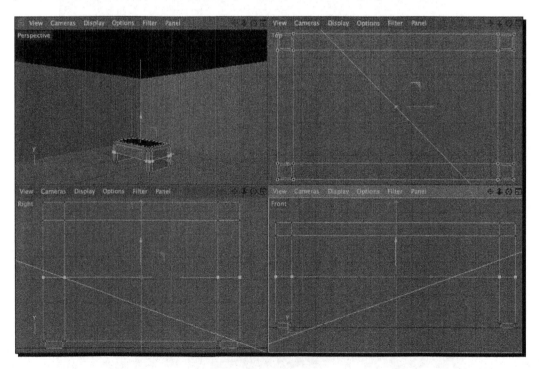

Also, if you feel this default view is too wide for the level of work we're currently doing, feel free to create new cameras or adjust the one we currently have. Switch to the four-camera mode and move along the appropriate axis in the **Top** camera, or simply reframe while the camera is selected in the viewport.

Pop quiz – reviewing our toolset

We've introduced a lot of concepts in this chapter that will become second nature as we move forward. Let's quickly review some of them!

Q1: We're working with a complex scene and would like to view an object from our current camera's perspective, but there's another object blocking it in our environment. Without switching cameras, how can we temporarily hide the foreground object?

Q2: We've created an object whose face is subdivided into five sections along the y axis and need to ensure that the center section is uniformly 15-cm wide. Which tools would we use to select this group of polygons?

Q3: We need to create a basic flagpole with a flat square base and a tall center pole. Which tools would we use to create this model?

Have a go hero – creating a light fixture

Extrude and **Inner Extrude** will be two of the most commonly used commands in your modeling skillset. In our last exercise, we took a simple cube and turned it into a desk with a quick combination of these two tools. We'll repeatedly refer back to these commands even as we progress through new methods of modeling, so let's add some extra detail to our scene by creating a couple of new objects. The following screenshot can be used as a jumping-off point—this is a wall sconce, with a bracket created entirely using **Extrude** and **Inner Extrude**. Feel free to create anything that feels appropriate for your office—a side table, picture frames to hang on the wall, extra seating, and so on.

You may find that your models look too basic as they are, but remember that we'll be learning how to add texture and life to them when we explore materials in *Chapter 4, Materials and Shaders*. The following is a screenshot of a wall sconce:

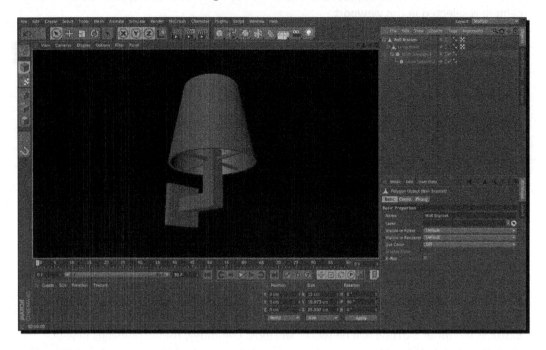

Summary

We're starting to get serious about modeling! So far, we've learned how attributes of various primitives differ, how to add only what we need and keep our models tidy, when to convert an object from parametric to polygonal, how to control points and faces on objects, and where our polygon commands are located and how to use them.

The next chapter will discuss modeling in a parametric way by combining new types of objects in order to achieve complex shapes quickly and easily. Even though we'll largely be looking at different methods of modeling, we'll be regularly returning to the foundation we've developed in this chapter.

3

Modeling Part 1: Splines, NURBS, Deformers, and Boole

In addition to polygon deformation, Cinema 4D provides a number of different ways to combine shapes into more complex geometry. We'll discuss the Cinema 4D NURBS objects and explore the built-in Spline menu, as well as discuss how to correctly export custom splines from vector software such as Adobe Illustrator. We'll discuss the hierarchy of parent/child relationships with regards to NURBS, deformers, and nulls and will take a closer look at the importance of hierarchy with regards to Boole objects. We'll use our new tools to create buttons and add details to our office.

In this chapter we will cover the following topics:

- ◆ Exploring the Spline menu
- ◆ Importing a spline from Adobe Illustrator
- ◆ Exploring NURBS objects
- ◆ Creating an organic model using HyperNURBS
- ◆ Applying deformers to primitives
- ◆ Learning additive and subtractive methods of modeling through booles and arrays
- ◆ Introducing null objects and understanding parent-child relationships

Before we begin

In *Chapter 2, Modeling Part 1: Edges, Faces, and Points*, we discussed multiple methods of modeling. We've explored how to move points and polygons to create unique shapes, but so far, we've focused on objects with a relatively rigid structure. In this chapter, we'll be using new techniques to create more organic objects.

We'll continue to refer back to some of the modeling principles we learned in *Chapter 2, Modeling Part 1: Edges, Faces, and Points*, as we progress through our animation. In this chapter, we'll learn methods that build on those principles and provide us with a complete model to texture and light up in the chapters to come.

If you have a copy of Adobe Illustrator, we'll be using it to create a custom spline and import it into our scene. If you don't have Illustrator, the steps are very similar within any other 2D vector drawing application. Splines can be drawn within Cinema 4D as well, but the controls are more primitive than those in Adobe Illustrator or a comparable program.

Understanding NURBS objects

One of the most important—and certainly quickest—methods of modeling in C4D is NURBS modeling. **NURBS (Non-Uniform Rational B-Splines)** modeling is a common thread among pieces of 3D software, created as a way to approach curves and organic forms in a digital world that speaks in hard lines and defined geometry. If you're familiar with vector tools in 2D software such as Adobe Illustrator, NURBS are the 3D equivalent of editing a Bezier curve. We begin with a series of points in space and use modifiers to shape them into the curves we want.

All 3D software applications approach the process a little differently, but C4D's approach generally starts with taking a spline and assigning it a behavior, whether that's following another spline or reacting to a point in space based on parameters we define. The most important types of NURBS objects are as follows:

♦ **HyperNURBS**: HyperNURBS are the most complex type of NURBS object. These objects take simple, low-poly models and smooth out their geometry to create a curved surface dependent on the parameters you supply, either through weighting edges or points or by providing additional geometry as a guide. HyperNURBS are similar to a lump of clay stretched out to try and fill a wire frame—you supply a series of key points, and C4D will interpret a continuous, smooth shape from them. The following is a screenshot of a HyperNURBS object:

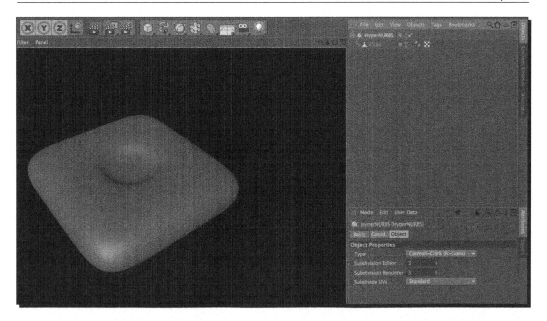

- ◆ **Lathe NURBS**: True to their name, they are easily remembered as anything you might create on a pottery wheel. Vases, glasses, and so on can be constructed by creating a 2D spline and rotating it around a center point, as shown in the following screenshot:

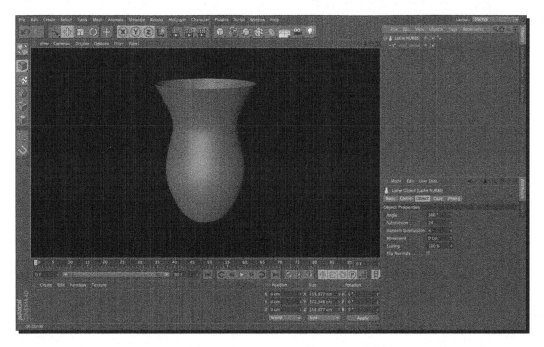

◆ **Sweep NURBS**: These are used when you need to add thickness to a spline—railings, rings, and so on. It is created from two splines—a contour spline and a path spline. So, for instance, if you are creating a railing on a staircase, you would create a 2D spline defining the angle and shape of the railing, then create a second circular spline representing the cross section and literally sweep it along the first path, as shown in the following screenshot:

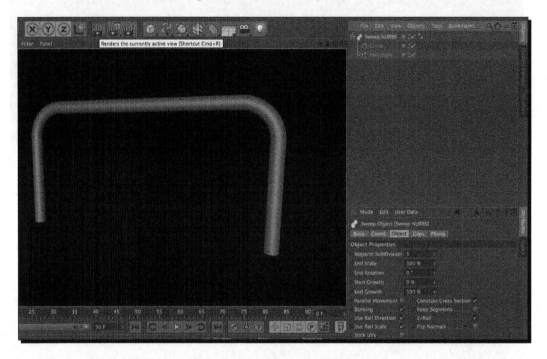

◆ **Extrude NURBS**: These are the simplest type of NURBS objects, creating geometry from just one 2D spline and moving it in any (or all three) direction(s). This object works similarly to the Extrude command we introduced in *Chapter 2, Modeling Part 1: Edges, Faces, and Points*, but creates an entire object instead of modifying part of an existing object, as shown in the following screenshot:

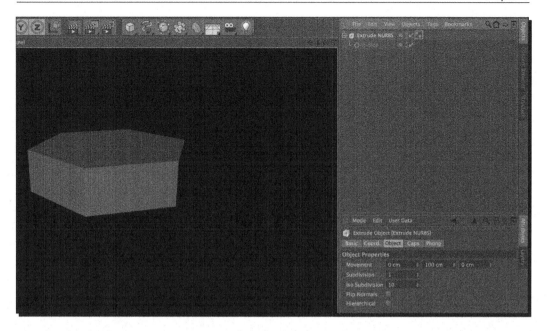

◆ **Loft NURBS**: This creates geometry across a series of cross-section splines and works well for many complex objects such as flower petals and canoes. The following screenshot shows a comparison of the final rendered image, the splines from which the object is created, as well as the full geometry of the NURBS object:

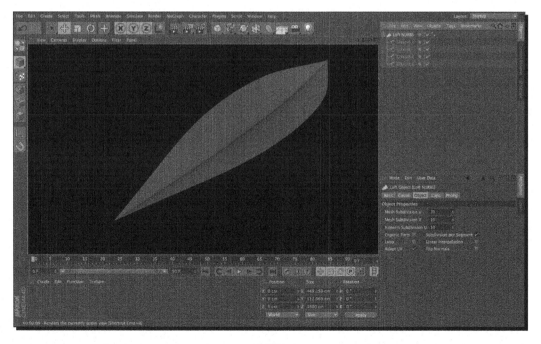

The next screenshot compares three variations of the same image—the wireframe of the Loft NURBS object shown previously, the splines used to create the Loft NURBS object, and the final rendered object:

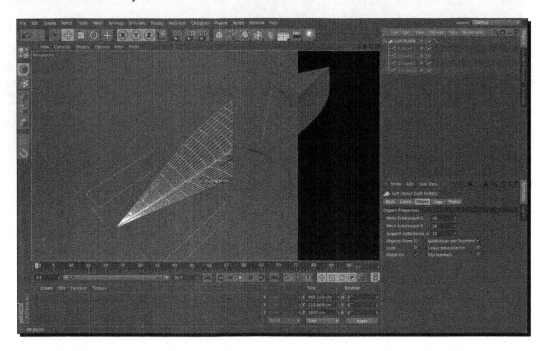

Exploring the Spline menu

Since many of our NURBS objects begin with splines, it's important to know the options for creating them. Our three basic options are as follows:

- **Using a pre-made spline**: This is a very good starting point, particularly for more rigid, symmetrical structures.

- **Creating a spline in C4D**: Freehand, Bezier, B-spline, and so on are all options.

- **Creating a spline in a separate program such as Adobe Illustrator**: If you're already comfortable with another piece of vector software, this is often the best option. The vector controls in C4D are acceptable but somewhat rudimentary compared to the pen tool, and importing splines (as we will learn soon) is very easy.

The Spline menu is located in our top menu next to the Primitives icon, as shown in the following screenshot:

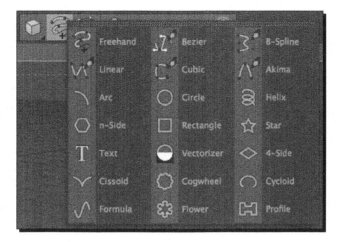

We'll explore these different spline types as we use them, but most of them are self-explanatory, and the icons are always there if you need a reference. Similar to the controls for primitives, when you've created a spline, all of the parameters exist in the Attributes Manager.

Time for action – creating and importing a spline

In this exercise, we're going to create a vase to sit on our desk using a Lathe NURBS object. We'll begin in Adobe Illustrator, but you can also create this spline within C4D or another drawing application. If you do create a spline within C4D, for this purpose, it's best to use either a Bezier spline or a B-spline to ensure a smooth curve.

1. To understand how the Lathe NURBS object works, let's quickly create an object before we make our spline, so that we can understand how spline rotation works. If your room model is still open, quickly create a new file so you have a blank environment.

2. Open the Spline menu and click on **4-Side**. Don't worry about changing its size; we're just using it for a test.

3. With the spline selected, press *C* on the keyboard to make it editable.

4. In the Attributes Manager, uncheck the box labeled **Close Spline**, as shown in the following screenshot:

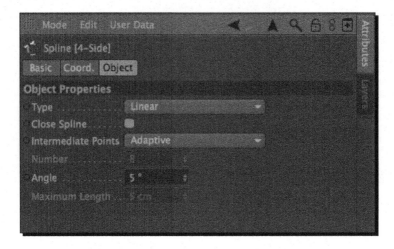

5. Switch to **Point Mode** and select the point on the right-hand side that is only connected to one other point, as shown in the following screenshot:

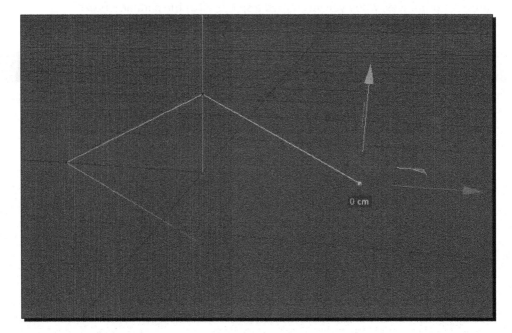

6. Delete this point, leaving only two sides to our spline.

7. Create a **Lathe NURBS** object.

8. Click-and-drag the **4-Side** spline to hover over the **Lathe NURBS** object in the Objects Manager. When a white outlined box with a down-pointing arrow above it pops up next to the cursor, release the object. In the future, we'll refer to this as creating a parent-child relationship—we have made the spline a child of the **Lathe NURBS** object, as shown in the following screenshot:

Now, our spline has revolved around itself and created a 3D object, as can be seen in the following screenshot:

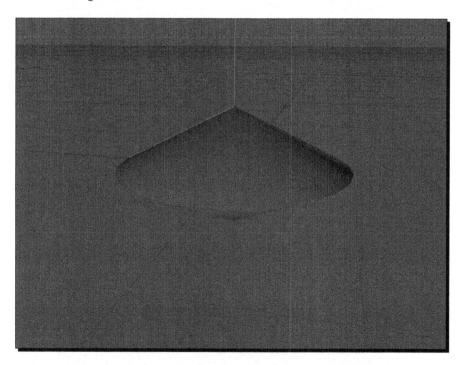

9. Let's experiment with the object we've made. Make sure you've switched back to **Object Mode** from **Point Mode**. With the spline selected (not the Lathe NURBS), select the **Move** tool and move it along the X axis. As you drag it away from the center point, you'll notice a hole opening in the model. This is because our **Lathe NURBS** object is located at (0,0,0). Our spline is told to rotate around its parent's center point, so even if we move the spline away, the rotation center remains the same. Note that if you move the **Lathe NURBS** object instead of the spline, the entire object will move as one instead of affecting the geometry of the object. This behavior affects all parent-child relationships within C4D; if you move the highest-level object, everything that is attached to it will move uniformly, but if you move one of the children, it does not affect the other objects in the scene. Our model should now appear like the following screenshot:

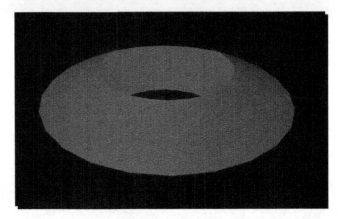

10. In the rendered view, you'll notice that our geometry is very segmented and choppy. In order to smooth it out, select the **Lathe NURBS** object and change the **Subdivision** value to a higher number. To test, **60** should be sufficient. Your values should line up with the following screenshot:

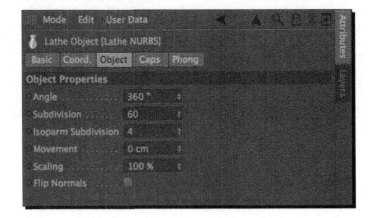

Move the 4-side spline back to (0 cm, 0 cm, 0cm) and render the viewport. Now our model is connected and smooth, as shown in the following screenshot:

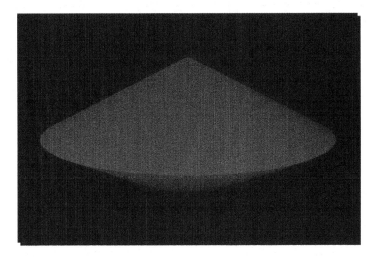

What just happened?

We've learned how parent-child relationships function within C4D, and we've also started to understand how NURBS objects are created. When we created our desk in *Chapter 2, Modeling Part 1: Edges, Faces, and Points*, we started with geometry, sliced it up, and pushed pieces around to make it into the form we wanted. Using our new method of modeling, we've taken a single spline, taught it to behave in a certain way, and created an entire object. Now that we've tested how the process works, let's make a real object that belongs in our office.

Time for action – creating a vase

In this exercise, we're going to create a vase to sit on our desk using Lathe NURBS. We'll begin in Adobe Illustrator, but you can also create this spline within C4D or another drawing application. If you do create a spline within C4D, for this purpose, it's best to use either a Bezier spline or a B-spline to ensure a smooth curve.

1. Open a blank document in Adobe Illustrator. The composition size doesn't matter; we'll define the spline's size once we've imported it into C4D.

2. Using the pen tool, draw a spline that represents a cross-section of a vase. The style is up to you! You may want to use a photo as a reference image. We'll be able to edit this spline once we import it into C4D, but try and get it relatively accurate while still in Illustrator. You can use the following image as a reference image as well. The following screenshot shows a spline that will give some thickness to our object, but a simpler spline won't cause any problems as we move forward (do not close the spline):

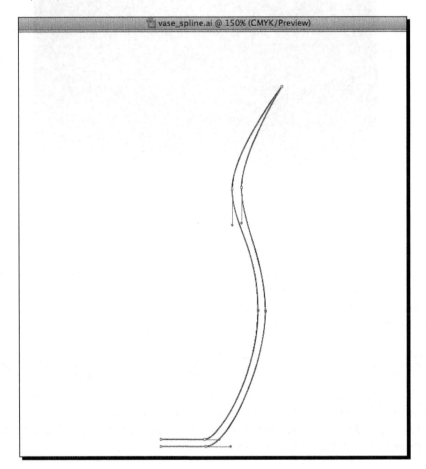

3. Navigate to **File** | **Save As...**, then set the file type to **Adobe Illustrator (AI)**. On the next dialog box, click on the drop-down menu at the top that defines which version of Illustrator you want your file to be in. By default, it should be set to whatever version you are currently using (in the next screenshot, **Illustrator CS5**).

4. Change the version to **Illustrator 8**. C4D is unable to import splines from newer versions of Illustrator. The following is a screenshot of the **Illustrator Options** window:

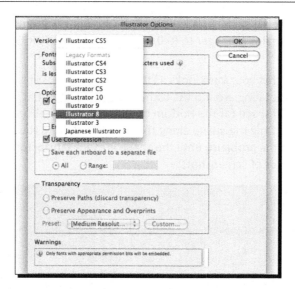

5. Close Adobe Illustrator and return to C4D. Select **File | Open** and navigate to your newly saved file. You will be presented with a **Scale** dialog box; click on **OK** to dismiss it, as we will make scale decisions once we've had a chance to work with our spline. Your spline should now appear in the Viewport, as shown in the following screenshot:

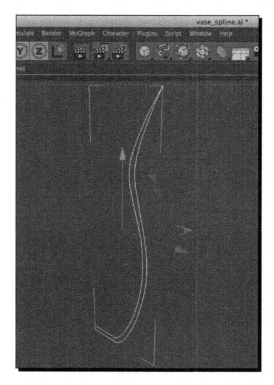

6. It is likely that the spline was imported at a strange position, so change the position in the Coordinates Manager to (0,0,0). Create a Lathe NURBS object and parent the spline to it.

7. Chances are that your vase looks a little strange and possibly narrow. This is because our spline is rotating around the Lathe NURBS object, set at the same position, and we've allotted space for the bottom of the vase that's being ignored due to the rotation axis. Drag the spline along the X axis (shifting to the **Front** camera may help you visualize the problem) until the shape is more satisfactory. This is shown in the following series of screenshots:

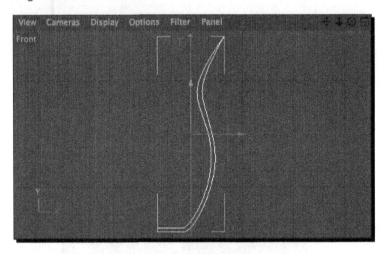

Our spline, on its own, currently overlaps the Y axis.

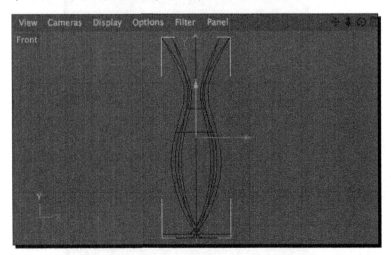

If the spline is not correctly centered, our vase creates a strange overlapping shape since C4D is attempting to revolve it around an incorrect center point.

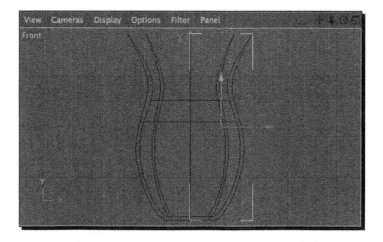

Moving the spline to the right on its X axis will create the desired shape.

8. It's almost time to add our vase to the office scene. With the **Loft NURBS** object and the **Scale** tool selected, begin scaling the object. It's okay to eyeball the dimensions; keep an eye on the Coordinates Manager and scale down until you reach around 30 cm on the Y axis. Depending on the curves in your object, you may want to increase the number of subdivisions on the Loft NURBS object. Remember that the higher the number, the smoother our model will be, but it also results in increased render time. We can always modify the value later. This is shown in the following screenshot:

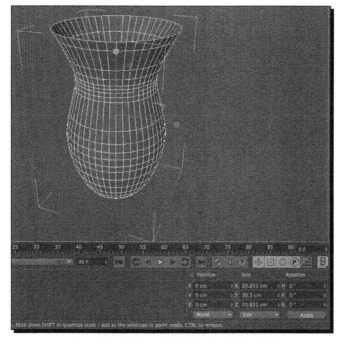

9. Copy the vase into your office model. Using multiple viewports, position it on your desk and scale as necessary if the proportion isn't appropriate to your environment. Our office model should now look like the following screenshot:

Time for action – creating a chair

Every office needs some place to sit, so let's combine a couple of things we've learned so far and pick up a couple of new techniques in order to create a modern chair to add to our office.

1. Let's first create the seat for the chair. Create a **Cube** object with dimensions (**55 cm**, **55 cm**, **2 cm**). Change the **Segments Y** field to **80**. This will give us enough geometry to make smooth curves on our seat, as shown in the following screenshot:

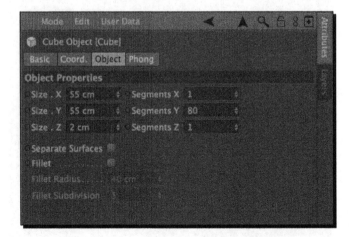

2. Click on the **Bend** icon to the right of the **NURBS** icon. If you click and hold on this icon, it will expand the entire Deformer menu as well. In the Objects Manager, make the Bend deformer a child of the cube we created in step 1. In the Attributes Manager, set **Size** to (10 cm, 10 cm, 50 cm) and **Strength** to 85. In the Coordinates Manager, rotate it to (90,0,-180). Your screenshot should appear like the following one:

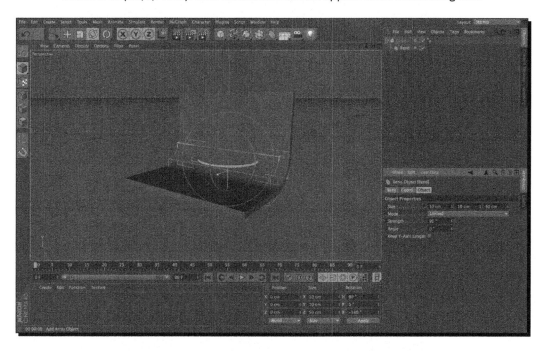

3. Create a cylinder with a radius of 1.5 cm and a height of 30 cm. Position it at (0 cm, -21 cm, -20 cm).

4. Create a **Cogwheel** spline.

5. Change its **Object Properties** to have a value of 5 in the **Teeth** field, **Inner Radius** and **Middle Radius** of 10 cm, and an **Outer Radius** of 30 cm on the **XZ** plane.

6. Position the spline at (0 cm, -36 cm, -20 cm):

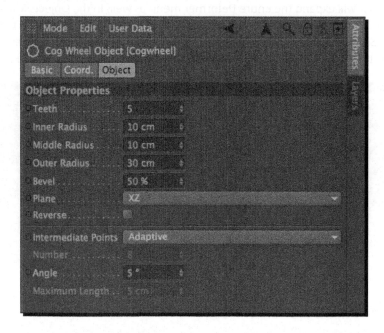

7. Create an **Extrude NURBS** object and set the cogwheel spline as its child. Set **Movement** of the NURBS object to (**0 cm, 1 cm, 0 cm**), as shown in the following screenshot:

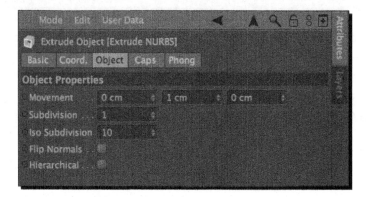

8. Click on the **Caps** tab and change the **End** cap to **Fillet Cap**, with **Steps** of **5** and a **Radius** of **0.5 cm**. In order to make the pieces look a little more similar, let's select our Cube (the seat of the chair) and check the Fillet box, with a **Radius** of **0.5 cm** and a **Subdivision** of **5**, as follows:

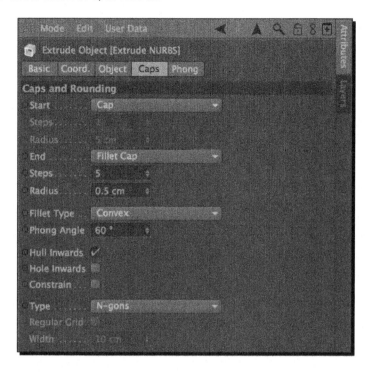

9. Create a sphere with a radius of 1.5 cm. Leave the segments at 24 for now; these will be the casters on the bottom of the chair and since we won't ever be terribly close to them, we can leave their geometry at the standard setting. If we need to reduce geometry later due to render time, we can always reduce the segments then.

10. Create an Array by clicking on the icon to the right of the **HyperNURBS** icon. In the Objects Manager, set the sphere we just created as a child of the Array. Change its position to (0 cm, -37.5 cm, -20 cm), with a radius of 27 cm and 4 copies. Check the **Top** view; the array should have evenly distributed the copies of the casters so that they line up with the arms of the cogwheel spline, as shown in the following screenshot:

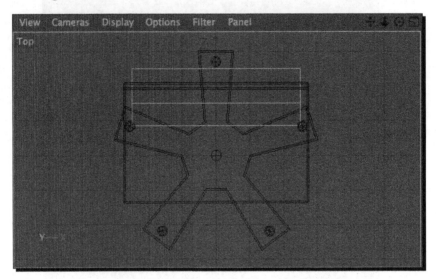

11. Select all objects in the scene and press *Option + G* on the keyboard. This groups (or parents) all objects to a null object, so there is one axis to control our whole chair. When multiple objects are linked to a single null, their position, scale, and rotation can be changed uniformly. Select the null object and change the Y position to 24.5 cm. This should put the bottom of the casters at 0 cm on the Y axis, so it will sit on our floor when we copy it into our office scene.

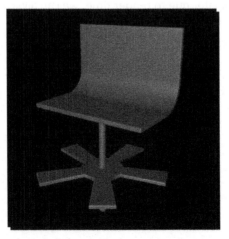

12. Rename the null object to Chair, then copy and paste it into the office scene. Position it appropriately facing towards the desk. Now our office is starting to come together, as shown in the following screenshot:

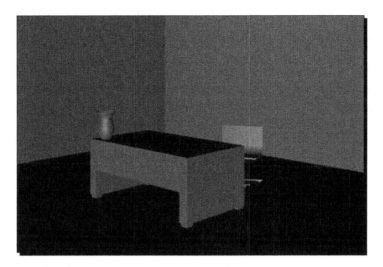

What just happened?

The process that we used to create our chair is the sort of process you should always keep in mind as you model. It's typical to default to certain tricks and techniques that you're more comfortable with, but it's usually a combination of tools that will get the job done quickly and most efficiently. In order to create a desk chair, we combined deformers, NURBS objects, primitives, and arrays. It's possible to create an entire complex model with just one technique, but often the strongest models come out of interesting combinations.

Have a go hero – using NURBS objects

We've used Extrude NURBS and Lathe NURBS, and we've looked at how Loft NURBS and Sweep NURBS work as well. Let's give our scene a little extra detail by using these object types to quickly create additional objects for our scene. You can create a picture frame for the wall or the desk with Extrude NURBS or Sweep NURBS, or a rug for the floor with Loft NURBS, or anything your imagination dreams up! Adding little details such as light switches and electrical sockets goes a long way towards creating realism in a scene.

HyperNURBS modeling

One of the best examples of combining polygonal models with more procedural techniques is HyperNURBS. As we've discussed earlier, all 3D software applications handle NURBS modeling a little differently. The HyperNURBS object is the closest that C4D actually gets to "true" NURBS modeling. By taking a low-poly model and understanding a couple of basic rules, you can create smooth, elegant models that will render beautifully.

HyperNURBS modeling is one of the trickiest concepts to master in C4D. Imagine a lump of clay sitting inside a simple wire frame. A HyperNURBS object creates a smooth form by taking that lump of clay and stretching it equally between all points on the frame. So if your frame is a simple eight-point cube, the HyperNURBS object will look like a sphere, because it is attempting to spread itself between those eight points equally.

There are two basic methods to "guide the clay" in a HyperNURBS model, as follows:

- Manually creating additional geometry to guide the form
- "Weighting" points and edges within your HyperNURBS object to tell C4D that it should stretch more in one specific direction

In this book, we'll be using the first method, which often proves more versatile for less organic modeling such as the structures we're creating in our office. Weighting requires a little bit of pre-planning, because if you want to further modify the base model after you've dropped it into a HyperNURBS object, you may get lost in trying to overcorrect for the earlier weighting decisions you've made. Let's create some additional furniture for our office and explore how to tailor geometry within the HyperNURBS system.

Time for action – using HyperNURBS objects

In this exercise, we'll create guest chairs to sit in front of our desk.

1. Create a new document and then create a cube with dimensions (**50 cm**, **4 cm**, **50 cm**) and subdivide their sides into (**3**, **1**, **3**), as shown in the following screenshot:

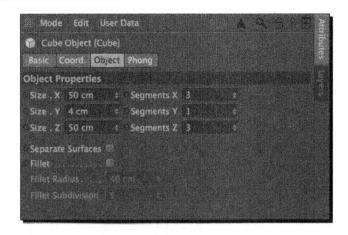

2. Make the cube editable (by pressing *C* on your keyboard), then switch from **Object Mode** to **Polygon Mode**. Using the **Loop Selection** tool, select one of the two center rings of polygons and change their width to 42 cm. Repeat this step with the other center ring until your model looks like the following one:

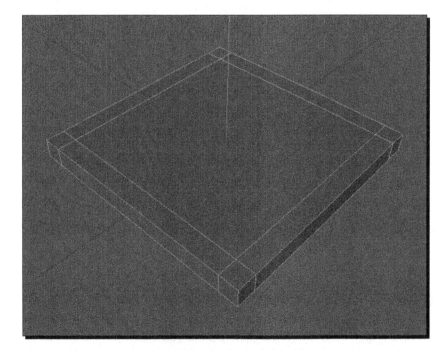

3. Select an outer-U shape of polygons on the top of the cube (without one of the long center pieces). Using the **Extrude** command, extrude them with an offset value of 30 cm. You should get the following screenshot:

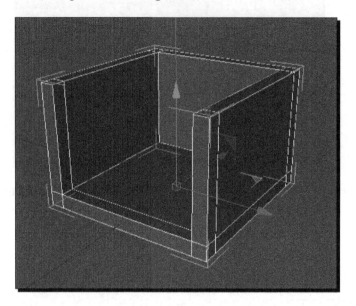

4. Create a HyperNURBS object and set the model you've been working on as a child of it. Click on **Render** and your screen should appear similar to the following screenshot:

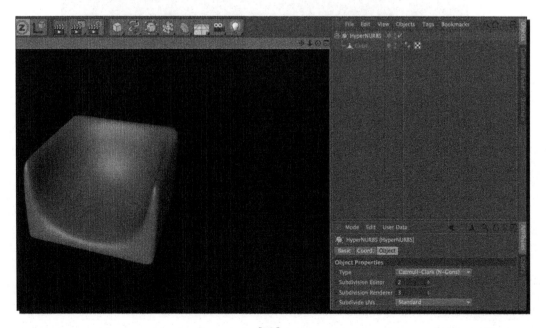

5. The model we've created so far is similar to what we're looking for, but not quite there yet. The arms are a little thin and we'd like to give a slightly more ergonomic look to it. The first step is to give ourselves some extra polygons, so let's select the **HyperNURBS** object and change the **Subdivision Editor** and **Subdivision Renderer** values to 4. This will dramatically increase our polygon count. We may decide that we want it to be lower when we move it into our scene, but for now, let's make the model as smooth as we can get it. Changing this value smoothens out the geometry, but still doesn't yield the comfortable-looking result we want. Our guest chair should now appear similar to the following screenshot:

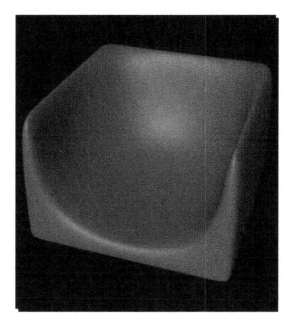

6. If you click on the green checkmark next to the **HyperNURBS** object, you'll notice that the smooth geometry disappears and we're back at our base model. Click and hold on the **Live Selection** icon at the top-left corner of the screen, and select **Rectangle Selection**. In the Attributes Manager, uncheck the box that says **Only Select Visible Elements**. Switch to **Point Mode**, then switch to the **Front** camera and drag a rectangle around the center two columns of points, as shown in the following screenshot:

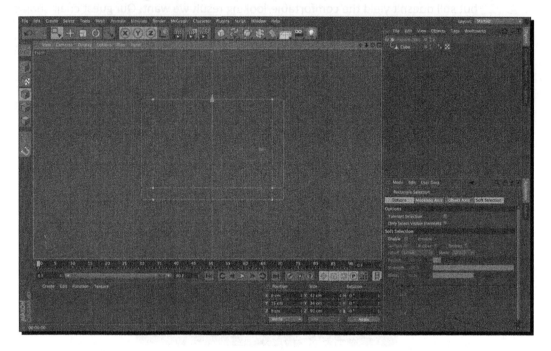

7. Click on what is now a red cross mark next to the **HyperNURBS** object (where the green checkmark once was) to view the HyperNURBS object again, then switch back to the **Perspective** camera. Try changing the width of these points to 36 cm instead of 42 cm. You can modify this value until you achieve a visually pleasing appearance.

8. Continue to modify the shape in this way by turning the **HyperNURBS** object on and off, and switching to various non-perspective cameras (you will want to remain symmetrical, that is if you move one side's value to -21 cm, move the other side to 21 cm) until you have an organic, comfortable shape for your chair. The following is a screenshot of a sample that you can strive for—the bottommost points are at -21 cm and 21 cm respectively, the topmost points are at -23 cm and 23 cm, and the center edge at the base of the chair has been modified to be only 30-cm wide:

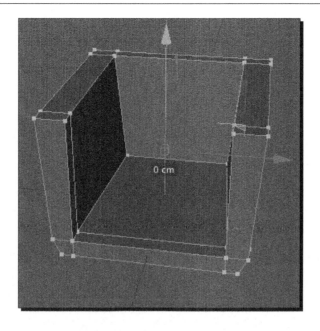

This will create a slightly more organic, more realistic shape, as shown in the following screenshot:

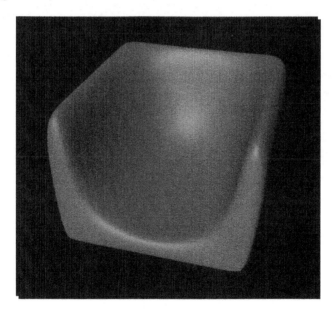

9. Move the HyperNURBS object to 36 cm on the Y axis. Create a cube with dimensions (3 cm, 36 cm, 3 cm) and change its position value to (-20 cm, 18 cm, 20 cm). Create three copies of this cube and change their X and Z values so that there are four evenly spaced legs, that is, alternate values of -20 and 20 on these axes. Then, group all objects under **Null**.

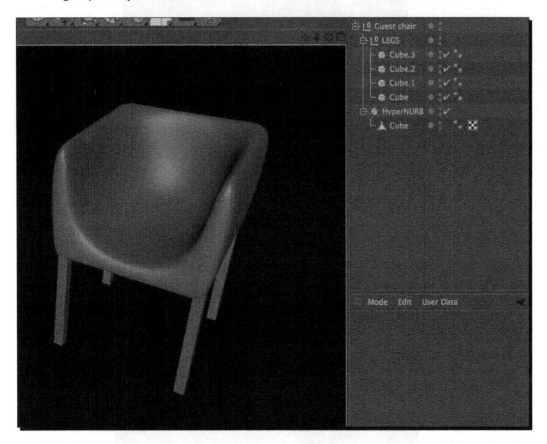

10. Copy this **Null** and paste it into the office scene. Rotate and position it accordingly in front of the desk, then make a copy and change its position to match. Our office model should appear similar to the following screenshot:

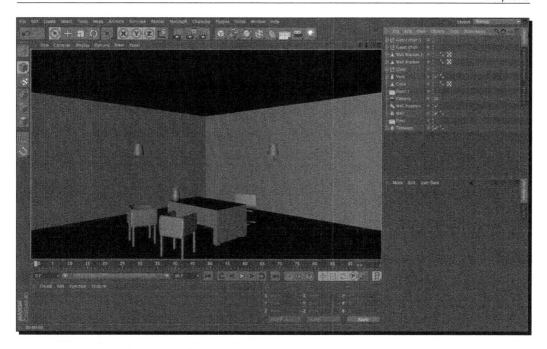

What just happened?

We've learned how to control objects on point and polygon levels, and now we're able to use those techniques to create smooth geometry with a HyperNURBS object. Remember that HyperNURBS can only predict your intended shape from the geometry you give it, so don't be afraid to add additional polygons as necessary.

Summary

At this point, we've got an excellent base model of an office that we can continue to use for texturing, lighting, and rendering. Also we've learned how to effectively create splines and utilize NURBS objects, how to apply deformers to basic objects to transform them into more complex geometry, and how to use HyperNURBS with basic polygonal models to create organic forms.

Moving forward, we won't be adding many more geometric details, so you may want to take the principles we've learned so far and add additional models to your scene. The next chapter will conquer materials and texturing to add life to what we've made so far!

4

Materials and Shaders

Now that we've got our model, it's time to make it look complete. We'll explore the process of making materials from scratch, as well as how to effectively use Cinema's built-in shaders. We'll examine the properties of materials like metal, glass, and wood and discuss how to effectively recreate real-world materials using material channels.

In this chapter we will:

- ◆ Explore each of the material channels
- ◆ Explore the pre-built shaders
- ◆ Apply materials to objects
- ◆ Discuss projection methods
- ◆ Create a selection set to assign multiple materials to objects

Before we begin

This chapter will use the office model we created in *Chapter 2, Modeling Part 1: Edges, Faces, and Points* and *Chapter 3, Modeling Part 1: Splines, NURBS, Deformers, and Boole*. We'll be taking a look at all of the things you need to know about materials, but will only be using the models we've made so far as examples. If you followed the advice at the end of *Chapter 3, Modeling Part 1: Splines, NURBS, Deformers, and Boole*, and added additional models to your scene, you'll be responsible for texturing those using the principles we explore in the rest of this chapter. Let's open our scene and get started!

Understanding materials

The words material and texture are often used interchangeably in 3D modeling. Take a look at the room around you. Every single object you see has texture, from a hardwood floor to a metal picture frame to a glass window to a matte plastic cup. Adding a material to an object in Cinema 4D helps to set it apart from the other objects around it. Materials define everything about the look and feel of an object outside of its basic geometric form. Our eyes are trained to understand the visual properties of texture by the way light plays on an object, so in 3D software, we manually define those properties through texture. Glossy or matte, colorful or grayscale, transparent or opaque – all of these parameters are controlled through materials.

Understanding material channels

The Materials Manager can be found underneath the Viewport in Cinema's Standard Layout. If you navigate to **Create | New Material** (or double-click anywhere in the Materials Manager), a box will pop up that contains a light gray sphere and is titled **Mat**, as follows:

This sphere represents our new material. You can change the sphere to a different shape such as a cube, torus, or flat shape by selecting a material and right-clicking on its icon in the Attributes Manager. Since not all materials in a scene will just be applied to spheres, it can be helpful to represent certain materials on a more appropriate shape. The name is **Mat** by default; if you double-click again, you should have a new material called Mat.1, with the next being Mat.2, and so on. If you select a material, its properties will appear in the Attributes Manager. Double-clicking on the material will create a new pop-up window, if you're working on a smaller screen or just want a resizable window. Just like renaming our objects as we create them in order to keep things tidy as we build more complex scenes, it is good practice to rename your materials as you create them. If you know you're creating a material that will be used for one specific object, correlating its name to the name of the object will make it easier for you to locate that material later.

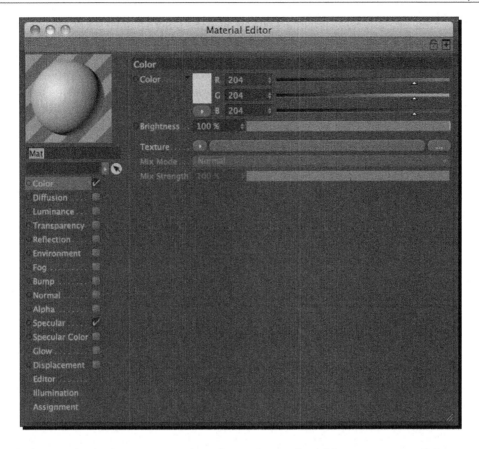

By default, two channels are activated—**Color** and **Specular**. This creates a very light gray object with a neutral level of shine.

The left column shows all of the channels you can add to a material. As a best practice, keep materials as simple as possible, only adding what you need. Every additional channel will slightly increase render time, so you may need to reduce settings if your renders become too time-consuming. Reflection and blur add a significant amount of time due to their need to compute the interaction with other objects in the scene, so make sure to use them only as necessary. Certain channels will be more commonly used than others, and we won't have an opportunity to explore all of them as we texture our model, but let's briefly examine some of the channels and how we would use them.

With very few exceptions, all materials should have the **Color** channel. The **Color** channel allows you to specify a color value for an object. The default color mode is RGB, but clicking on the arrow underneath the color preview allows you to select another color mode. This is particularly useful if you are texturing a model for a company or another purpose that gives you specific values for a product—style guides traditionally specify an RGB value to ensure consistency across branding. However, in these instances, it's important to remember that color is subjective and depends on the lighting in the scene, so it may be necessary to tweak the value accordingly to overcompensate.

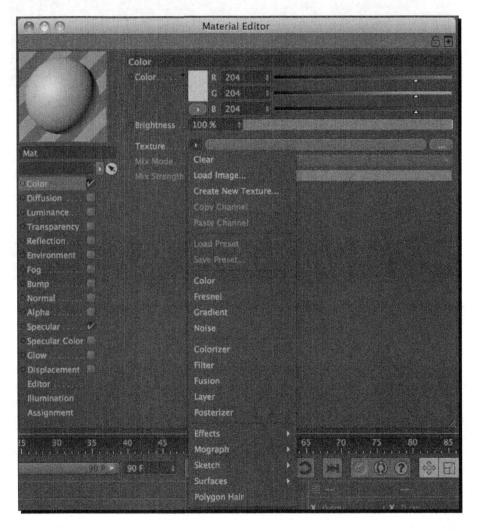

Certain aspects of a material's appearance can be controlled procedurally (by generating all of their properties within C4D, such as a painted wall or a wooden floor), or controlled by external images (such as a logo or an outdoor image behind a window). So, for example, if you need to add a logo to a product, click on the arrow to the right of **Texture** (as shown in the preceding screenshot) and select **Load Image....** This will allow you to attach a photo to a texture. The simplest application for this is in the **Color** channel, but as we learn a little more about how to build materials, we'll discuss additional options.

Also in the drop-down menu, you'll see a variety of options that will either replace the standard color value or add to it. Many of these, particularly **Surfaces**, will be useful as we texture our scene. Surfaces will allow you to generate textures such as tiles and planks without loading in an external image, ensuring higher quality without any pixelation, as well as easier customization down the line:

The **Diffusion** channel creates additional dimension by affecting the behavior of the **Color** channel. This allows you to add slight variations on the surface of an object by simulating irregularities such as dirt or scratches.

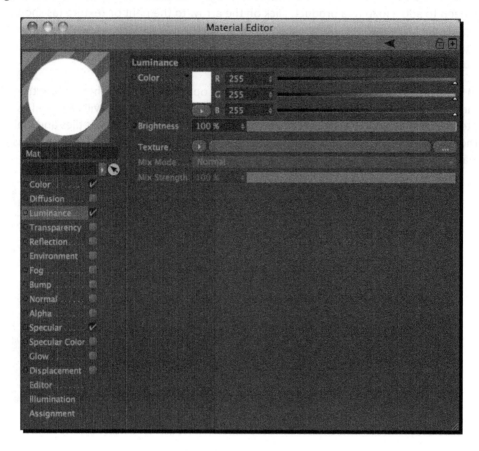

Luminance allows you to create self-illuminated objects. The default **Brightness** value is **100%**, but lowering this value allows for some interesting effects. **Luminance** overrides the color channel at 100 percent brightness, which makes it function independently of any lights in the scene. At lower values, it will mix with the color channel. This can be an interesting tweak if you're working on the lighting for a scene and need an object to be brighter but don't want to disturb the rest of the environment; adding a low luminance value to a material can make your whites brighter! This is not quite the same as turning an object into a light, however, as the material will only affect neighboring objects under very specific circumstances.

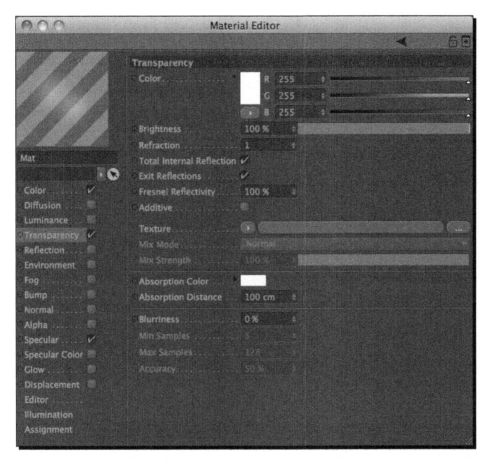

Transparency allows you to control the opacity of an object. By default, the **Brightness** level is set at **100 %**, creating a completely transparent object. **Transparency** is one of the more complex channels, because transparent objects have a variety of properties in addition to just being see-through. The most important value to change is **Refraction**. **Refraction** is a measure of how light bends through the surface of an object. A simple web search for "Refraction index" will turn up many charts with known values for transparent values, however, much like color, there may be some tweaking to do to make your object behave correctly. Changing the **Refraction** value from **1** to **1.52** will create a glass texture that looks much more realistic than the texture shown previously:

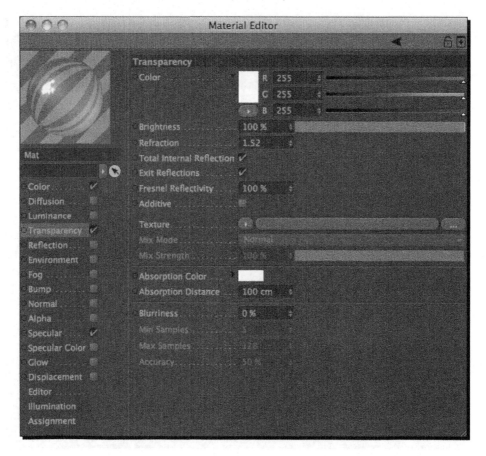

Similar to the Color channel, you can also add an image, as well as control the **Absorption Color** and **Blurriness**. Take a look at everything around you: a fork, your desk, the edge of your computer monitor, a plastic cup. All of these objects are reflecting light, and you can most likely get a sense of the world around them and how they fit in by those interactions. A shiny object sitting next to a matte object will pick up some of the matte object's properties, and vice versa. However, a pure reflection (like what you see in a clean mirror) is rare to come by. Most of the objects around you get some sort of reflection, but we can identify an object as shiny or matte based on just how blurry that reflection is. Blurry attributes are one of the easiest ways to add realism to a texture, however, they are also responsible for much, much higher render times. If you add blurriness to materials, make sure to set the **Max Samples** only as high as you need for the quality level you desire. Keeping this value low will go a long way in controlling render time:

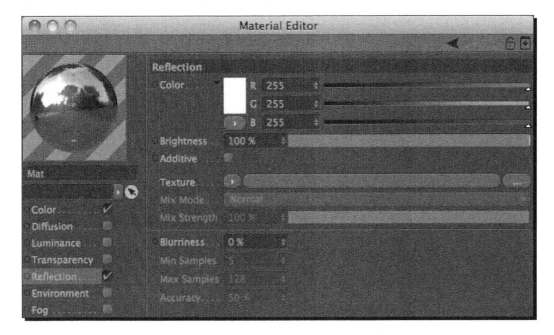

Most objects have some level of reflection in 3D space, however, reflections increase the render time considerably, so it's up to us to decide whether or not that reflection is needed to create a realistic image. When you enable the **Reflection** channel, its default 100 percent value turns our object into a perfect mirror. You may be surprised at how low you can set your brightness level and still achieve a tremendous amount of reflection. A small blurriness value will often be helpful depending on how prominent the object is in your scene. Without any blurriness, reflections will be perfectly mirrored, which may not look realistic. Don't worry too much about setting your reflection values if you're adding materials before lighting; the two will go hand-in-hand and you'll most likely have to change their values after your lighting setup is finished:

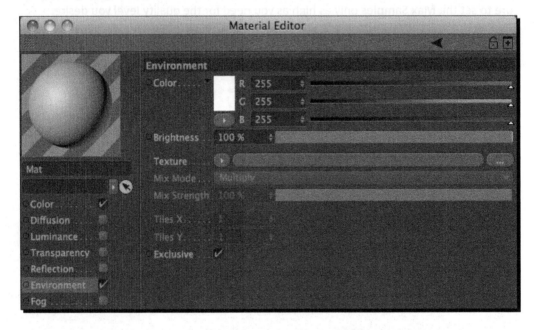

The **Environment** channel is used to simulate reflection in scenes that are not set up with enough supporting objects. For example, if you are creating a render of a piece of metal jewelry, you want to reinforce the reflective nature of the object, but you may not want to build an entire environment for it. Adding texture through the **Environment** channel allows you to create fake reflections to add realism to your renders:

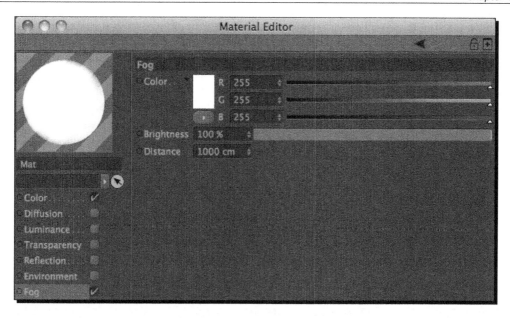

The **Fog** channel fills your object with fog, which can be used to create interesting environmental effects. As you work, you will most likely find that your opportunities to use the fog channel are limited; however, it can be very effective for adding fog to a specific area of your scene. Imagine an outdoor scene with fog in the distance; this is a great opportunity to create a low-geometry object and fill it with fog to simulate low-hanging clouds:

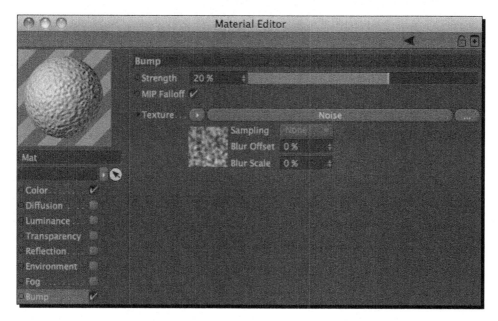

Adding the **Bump** effect to your material is an easy way to add dimension to the surface of an object. By adding a black and white image either procedurally in Cinema or via an image created externally, the surface geometry of an object is distorted at render time without actually creating additional points and faces. A 100 percent white area of an image will represent the highest extrusion on an object, while 100 percent black areas will be the most indented (if you ever forget and accidentally reverse the two, you can easily overcompensate for this by adding a negative percentage in the **Strength** field). This can be very useful for generating textures like brick and tile. The Normal effect works similarly, but works in all three directions (XYZ) instead of just two, and uses an RGB color mode to generate surface distortion instead of black and white:

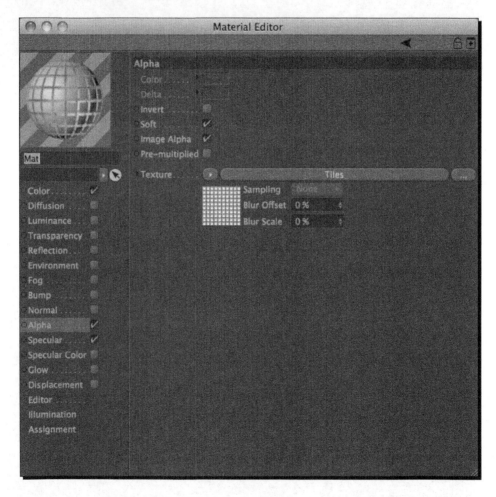

The **Alpha** channel takes its name from a concept that is standard across many pieces of animation and design software. Similar to **Bump**, **Alpha** uses a black and white image model that affects the visual appearance of an object—in this case, by creating transparency—without creating additional geometry. As you can see in the previous screenshot, we've added a black and white tile texture in the **Alpha** channel, which removes the black areas of the image and projects only the white areas. This allows you to create the look of complex objects without creating complex geometry. It is a two-dimensional effect, however, that does not project geometry; so applying a flat texture of a tree with an alpha channel onto a plane will mean that if the camera approaches too close to the object, its lack of dimensionality will become noticeable:

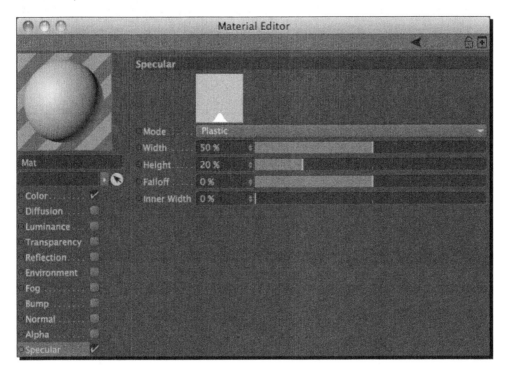

The **Specular** channel defines the behavior of highlights. As you can see in the following screenshot, adjusting the **Width**, **Height**, **Falloff**, and **Inner Width** values can make an object look glossy or matte, without adding environment or reflection:

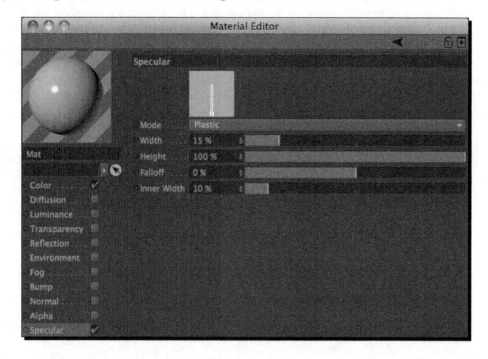

Most objects (unless there is a reason you don't want any highlights to appear on them whatsoever) should have the **Specular** attribute enabled:

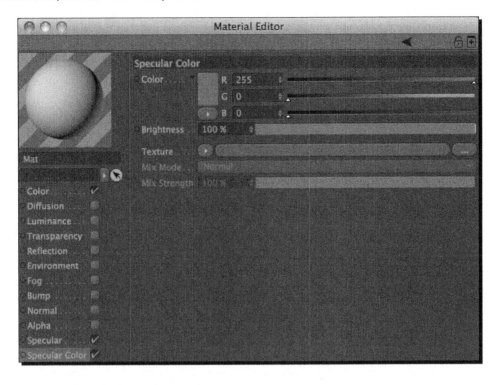

Specular Color allows you to add color to just the highlight on an object. As you can see in the previous screenshot, by adding a red highlight, the object is still the same light-gray as before, but the appearance is affected as if it is catching reflection off of a neighboring object. A red cup sitting next to a blue cup will appear mostly red, but if the cups are sitting close to one another, you will notice a small amount of blue spilling over to the red cup. This is easy to see in the real world, but processor-intensive to replicate in 3D space. **Specular Color** can be helpful when developing product renders and in reducing render time.

Glow adds a post effect that creates an artificial halo around objects as shown in the previous screenshot. The controls are relatively rudimentary and if you have additional post effects, it may not deliver the results you want. We'll discuss ways to create glowing objects by exporting layers in a later chapter.

Time for action – texturing our environment

To start creating our materials library, let's first make some base materials for our environment. If you don't already have your office scene open, go ahead and open it up, as we'll be spending this chapter adding texture to what we've created so far.

1. Create a new material by either double-clicking on the Materials Manager or by navigating to **Create | New Material**. This material will be for our wall. In the **Color** attribute, change the color to a value of your choice. The following example uses (150, 0, 0) to create a red wall.

2. Under the **Specular** attribute, change the **Height** value to **2 %**. This will create an almost entirely matte surface:

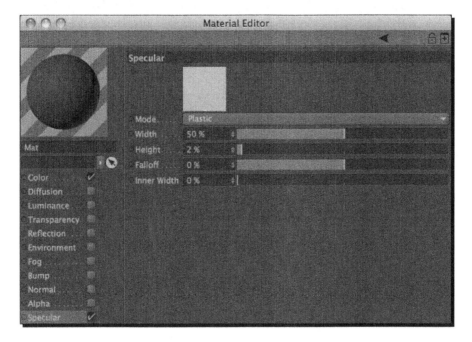

3. Drag-and-drop the material from the Materials Manager onto the object either in your Objects Manager or the Viewport. The Objects Manager allows you to make sure you're precise and is helpful in complex scenes, but if you haven't changed the names of objects as you go, the Viewport works just as well and allows you to select it visually. The color of your object should have changed in the Viewport, and a small version of the material icon should appear to the right of your object in your Objects Manager.

4. In *Chapter 2, Modeling Part 1: Edges, Faces, and Points*, we created our second wall as an instance of the first. Select the instance and press *C* on your keyboard to make it editable. This will ensure that the color we add to the other object is not projected onto both walls.

5. In the **Material Editor** window, select your material, then copy and paste it to make a duplicate. Change the color to something neutral—the following example shows (220, 220, 175). When we begin to add lighting in the next chapter, we may find that these colors need to be tweaked, but this will get us started.

6. Assign the same ivory material to the ceiling. Since there are no lights in our environment, it's impossible to tell if the color has actually changed. Click on the Light icon at the far right of the toolbar and create an omni light. We'll add additional lighting and learn about the parameters in the next chapter, but for now, move it to 200 cm on the Y axis. This should provide relatively even lighting in our room that will function as a work light for now.

What just happened?

We've set up our very first material! This will be the process we use for every material we create. If you're creating similar materials—like the two paint colors that we want to have the same finish—it's easiest to duplicate them and just make the necessary adjustments instead of starting over from scratch. As we move forward and create new materials, always keep their basic properties in mind, and you'll have realistic-looking scenes in no time!

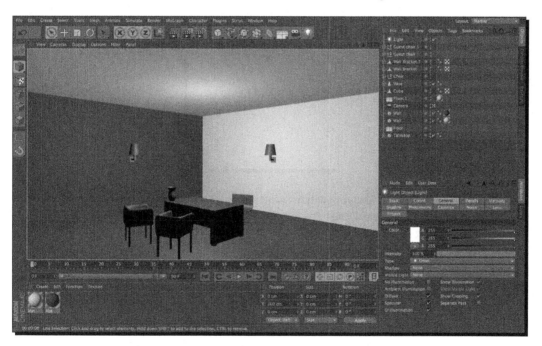

Have a go hero – adding details to our scene

Now that we've added a couple of materials to our scene, it looks like we could use a little more detail in our scene. We'll gain some realism when we add lighting and change some of our render settings, but adding a little detail to the geometry of our room will really help to set the scene. The following are a couple of suggestions to get you started:

- To make use of the ceiling mould and floor trim functions, create a rectangular spline the same size as the room. Now using a Sweep NURBS object, create a decorative trim or crown moulding for your office. Design your own detail, or create a spline similar to the following one. This spline would work well for moulding the ceiling, but floor trim is traditionally simpler:

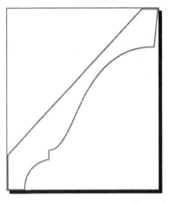

- Little details such as light switches and wall sockets go a long way to adding realism to a scene. Simple touches, for example adding an electrical cord to a floor lamp and plugging it in can do wonders!

- Select one of the walls and add a window to it. The easiest way to do this is by selecting one of the walls and adding it to a **Boole** object with another cube set as a child underneath it. The size and placement of the second cube will determine the size of your window. You can create a second window by setting it as a child to the first one. A **Boole** object functions entirely by subtracting one object from another, so if there are multiple objects to subtract, they must all be nested to a parent (putting them both within a null object works as well). Our office model will be similar to the following screenshot:

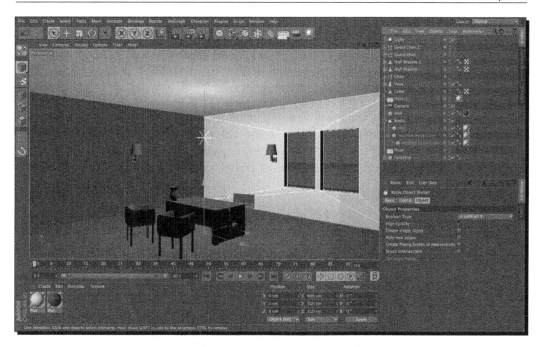

◆ Consider adding trim and a sill to the window. Every detail helps!

What just happened?

3D animation is rarely a perfectly linear process. As we added materials, we found that some areas of our scene are less visually interesting and just need a little more, so we've gone back and added a little visual interest by giving the model a little extra detail. For the purposes of this book, we've divided topics neatly into chapters, but in real life, you'll find yourself doing a lot of bouncing around. When we add lighting in the next chapter, we will likely need to revisit some properties of the materials we create, and when we modify our render settings, we may find ourselves needing to make additional modifications.

If you feel comfortable with modeling at this point, feel free to add additional detail—curtains, floor rugs, ceiling lights, and so on. We won't revisit modeling too much beyond this point, so the realism is up to you! Future screenshots may vary slightly from your current model, and you can use them as suggestions for additional objects to add to your scene. The best way to develop your 3D skills is with practice and variety, so go nuts!

Shaders

Cinema comes with a number of pre-built materials with slightly different attributes than the ones we've explored so far. These special materials are called **Shaders**, and can be found by navigating to **Create | Shader** in the Materials Manager.

Each shader's attributes are slightly different depending on the texture they emulate, so we won't examine each of them in great depth like we did with the more global attributes. We'll briefly list them here for reference, and in the next chapter, we'll use them to texture our model. These shaders are often very dependent on lighting, which makes it difficult to begin assigning them now.

The following list gives a description of all the general shaders, omitting special shaders used with modules such as Hair and Sketch:

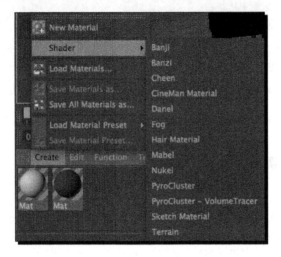

Your list may look slightly different than the following one depending on which package you have installed:

- **Banji**: Glass
- **Banzi**: Wood
- **Cheen**: An organic texture, helpful with microscopic and cellular objects
- **Danel**: Metal
- **Fog**: Self-explanatory
- **Mabel**: Marble
- **Nukei**: Rust
- **Pyrocluster**: Aids in particle generation; clouds, fire, and so on
- **Terrain**: Landscape

Time for action – additional textures

As mentioned, we'll go back and adjust things a little more once we've got our lighting plan set, but let's go ahead and set up the rest of our materials so we're ready to go as we polish the look of our scene.

1. First, let's add glass to the windows we created in the *Have a go hero – adding details to our scene* section in this chapter. The easiest way to do this is to select the wall (which should be the top object in the Boole), copy and paste it, and change its thickness to something small. You can resize the cube and align it better to the actual windows, but since it is hidden inside our wall anyway, it shouldn't matter. This is a key concept to get used to in 3D animation—model what you need to, and add details if necessary. In this case, we don't need it, but if we move a camera very close to it, we'll need to add additional detail. It's just a background environmental object at this point, so we can leave it as is (if your copied object has a material assigned to it, select the material tag and delete it at this time).

2. Create a new material and rename it to **Glass**. Under the **Basic** tab, check the **Transparency** box. Change the **Refraction** value to **1.52**—the refraction index for glass. Assign this material to the new object you created and rename the object to **Window Glass**.

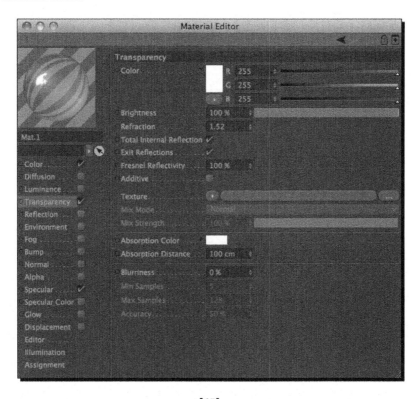

3. Create a new material for the trim around the windows, ceiling, and floor. If you look at the room around you, you may notice there is a difference in the paint finish used on the walls and any trim around doors, windows, and so on. Usually the finish on trim is slightly glossier, so we'll emulate that using the **Specular** value. Change **Color** to be pure white (**255, 255, 255**), then change the **Specular Width** to **25 %** and the **Height** to **100 %**.

4. Assign the new material to all trim objects in the room. When you do a test render of your scene, you may think this color is a little too bright; you can change it now, but remember that the lighting you set up will affect the color of objects a great deal.

5. Open up your **Render Settings** window by clicking on the rightmost icon of the three render icons in your top toolbar. Click on **Anti-Aliasing** on the left sidebar, then change **Anti-Aliasing** to **Best**. We'll learn more about render settings in the next chapter, but for now, this simple change will clear up some of the jagged geometry you may have seen on some of the straight lines.

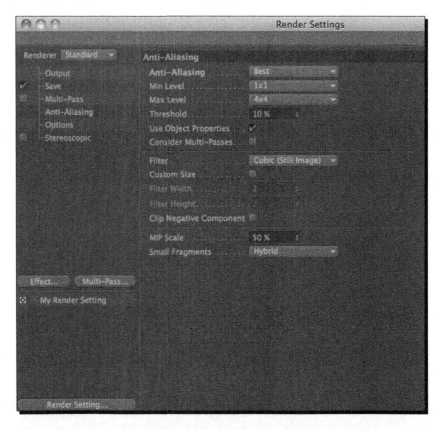

6. To create a texture for the floor, we'll load in an external image. You can also create wood grain procedurally. Many websites offer free textures for personal, non-commercial use. Search for something like "seamless wood textures", and make sure you choose an image that has decently high resolution—anything around 1000 x 1000 px should be sufficient. Choose something that looks like floorboards, parquet, and so on. Save it in the same directory as your .c4d file.

7. Create a new texture, and under **Color**, click on the three dots to the right of **Texture**. This will allow you to select the image from your hard drive. Then, assign the texture to the floor.

8. You may notice that your texture looks too large or too small in proportion to the floor. This can easily be resized. With the object selected, change into **Texture Axis** mode by selecting the second icon from the top on the left-hand side of the screen—it looks like a checkerboard on the side of a cube. In the Coordinates Manager, you can change the scale of the texture. Make sure you click on **Apply** to accept the changes. Then, test your render to double-check the scale. You should get a screenshot similar to the following one:

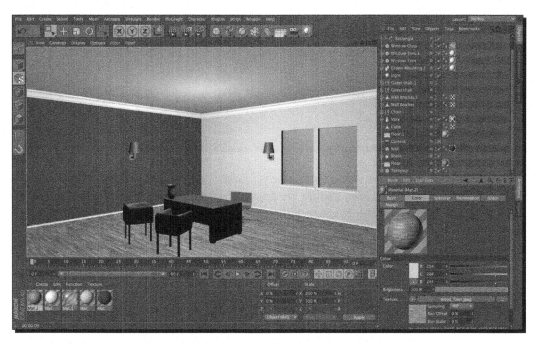

9. Next, we'll create a basic brown leather texture. Create a new material and change its color to a medium brown, the example will show (**115**, **90**, **65**). Then, activate the **Diffusion** channel. Click on the arrow to the right of **Texture** and select **Noise**. Double-click on the black and white image that appears under **Noise** and change the **Global Scale** to **1000 %**. Apply this texture to the two guest chairs to get a screenshot similar to the following one:

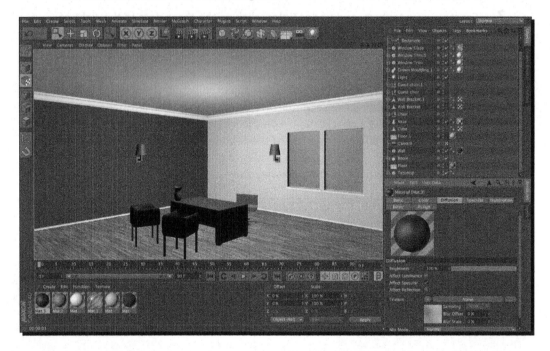

10. Using the materials we've created so far, continue to add texture to the rest of the room. A different wood texture would work well for the desk, and perhaps the desk chair is wood as well. The legs of the chairs could be wood or metal, and the flower pot could be glass, metal, or ceramic. Continue to experiment, and we'll discuss additional appropriate techniques in the next chapter.

Summary

We've explored the basic properties of materials in this chapter, but we'll continue to explore them as we move forward. So far, we've learned about the uses of each of the material channels, how to assign a material to an object, how to use external images to add realism to a scene, how to adjust the scale of a material, and uses for different types of shaders.

In the next chapter we will continue to explore materials as we add lights, shadows, and learn how to create beautiful images by changing our render settings.

5
Lighting and Rendering

We've created a textured model—now it's time to add lighting and an environment to create a usable end product. We've briefly touched on the Render menu in Chapter 1, Getting to Know Cinema 4D, but now we'll learn how to export still images and create the highest quality output possible in the shortest amount of time. Cinema 4D's Advanced Render module gives you limitless options for customizing your render. We'll determine what settings are most important, adjust our lights and materials as necessary, and prepare to move into animation.

In this chapter we will learn about:

- ◆ Types of lights
- ◆ Light settings such as brightness and shadow
- ◆ Falloff
- ◆ Techniques for how and where to use lights
- ◆ Anti-aliasing
- ◆ Global illumination
- ◆ Ambient occlusion
- ◆ Post effects
- ◆ Render options
- ◆ Render optimization

Before we begin

So far, we've created a model of an office that has geometry and texture. In this chapter, we'll bring it all together and create beautiful, realistic images.

Find a photograph and take a look at it. Consider all the things that are there to let you know that it's a real image—if it's an outdoor photo taken when it's sunny, perhaps it's the harsh shadows on the ground. If it's an indoor photo, maybe it's the softness at the corners of a room. Whatever your photo, the key to realism is consistency. Sunlight coming in from outside will give a warm glow to a room, regardless of whether or not it's shining directly on the window. All the shadows from one particular light source will be at the same angle, with smaller or wider shadows depending on the distance from the light.

This is a difficult concept to convey in drawing and 2D-based digital illustration, but much easier to accomplish in 3D software. When working on an abstract scene, your lights can be placed anywhere you want to achieve the look you're going for. On more realistic scenes such as our office, we should try our best to emulate real-world conditions. If you create a lamp and want it to be lit, make sure the light is angled in the same direction as the fixture. If you're able to look at a similar object near you, it's always good to closely observe it to make sure your 3D objects are behaving the same way.

As we move into lighting, make sure every object in your scene has a texture assigned to it. We may need to adjust some of the properties of our materials as we add lighting, but we'll figure that out as we go along. If you notice that a particular object has too much of a highlight or isn't quite the color you're looking for, consider the neighboring objects in the scene. If everything looks universally off, consider changing settings on the light, but if just one or two objects look strange, it may be an issue with their material. Let's dive in!

Exploring light settings

Select the placeholder light we created in our scene before texturing (if it hasn't been renamed, it will be called **Light**; if you did not create a light in the previous chapter, create one now by clicking on the light bulb icon at the far right of the tool palette). Take a look at the Attributes Manager. The light has the same **Basic** and **Coordinates** tabs that we've seen for our other objects, but the rest of the tabs are specific to lights only.

There are hundreds of individual settings that can be changed on each light, so we'll just look at the most common ones to get started. Let's start by selecting our light, then looking at the **General** tab in the Attributes Manager, as shown in the following screenshot:

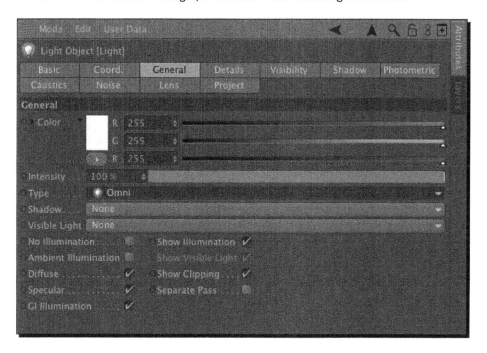

The **General** tab allows us to change some basic settings for our lights, such as color, brightness, and shadow. In the real world, the color of a light is dictated by temperature, measured in kelvins. Cinema determines light color entirely based on RGB values. A web search for "kelvin to RGB" will provide values for many everyday lighting situations, such as tungsten bulbs (255, 214, 170) versus halogen bulbs (211, 241, 224). Just like we discussed in *Chapter 4, Materials and Shaders*, lighting often needs to be overcompensated to look appropriate for the scene, even if you aren't using the exact RGB values that the real-world situation calls for. However, these values can be a good starting point.

It is often helpful to add a little bit of warmth or coolness to the color of your lights to simulate a real-world environment. The brightness of your light is determined by the **Intensity** value. The default value is 100 percent. You can enter values higher than 100 percent, but often you will find that if you need to go much above 100 percent, adding additional light sources may be the better idea.

The **General** tab is also where we determine what type of light we'll be using:

Types of lights in C4D include the following:

◆ **Omni**: This is short for omnipresent. It radiates light evenly in all directions from a single point. It is the default and most commonly used light type.

◆ **Spot**: This is a point light that will radiate light in one specific direction, in either a round cone (**Spotlight**), a square pyramid (**Square Spot**), a straight cylinder (**Parallel Spot**), or a straight cube (**Square Parallel Spot**).

◆ **Infinite**: This works similar to a parallel spot (shadow direction determined by the light's Z axis) but with a size that extends infinitely in the X and Y directions.

◆ **Area**: This is a light that radiates from a specific shape.

◆ **IES**: This is specific to the Visualize and Studio packages; IES lights allow you to import a specific light created by a manufacturer, usually available on their website. If you are working on an architectural scene and are creating a real-world visualization, you can use the vendor's models to create an exact replica of the lighting setup.

Under **Type**, you can turn on **Shadow**. In real life, all lights give off some sort of shadow. However, you may find that turning on shadows for all of your lights in a scene causes overlap that appears visually confusing, so there are some situations where you might want a light to not cast shadows. Soft shadows are what you will generally want to use, but hard shadows have their place as well—sunlight streaming in a window at a bright time of day is a good example. Change the shadow type to **Soft** and perform a test render to get the next screenshot:

The shadows here are currently too harsh and look unrealistic, but compare the previous screenshot with the following screenshot of our render, and you'll see that we're headed in the right direction:

Under the **Details** tab, you can set a **Falloff** value for your lights. In the real world, lights have an infinite falloff that follows a curve until the value of their effect on the environment effectively approaches zero. In 3D space, we define the distance from the light source where that zero point occurs. Change the **Falloff** value to **Inverse Square** and perform a test render:

Notice that our scene looks far too blown out. This is because our Falloff value is set too high—500 cm is the default setting, which is too large of a light source for our room. Change the value to 200 cm and see how it looks:

Our new result is much more appropriate for the scene. If you want your office a little brighter, you can always change the falloff value. Notice that the ceiling is too blown out; we'll revisit that problem a little later.

The additional tabs on your light such as **Visibility**, **Photometric**, **Caustics**, and so on all have advanced settings that can add realism and interesting lighting effects to your scene and should be explored on your own as you advance in your lighting techniques. The only additional tab we'll address here for now is **Shadow**. The biggest problem with our current render is that while the shadows are helping us add depth to our scene, they are too dark and harsh. Let's change the density to 75 percent and the color to RGB (38, 38, 38). This will result in semi-transparent shadows that are dark-gray instead of jet-black:

Now that we've explored some of the basic settings of lights, let's start giving more life to our scene!

Have a go hero – add an exterior environment

Looking at the previous screenshot we can say that one of the issues we face is the lack of outdoor environment. Select an outdoor landscape photo—one that you've taken perhaps—and create a material with it in the **Color** channel (as we discussed in the previous chapter, if you need to make it slightly brighter, you can always add it to the **Luminance** channel as well). Assign this material to a plane and place it outside the window.

Then, create a **Parallel Spot** and angle it so the light is spilling in through the window. Make sure to give it a hard shadow, and consider changing the color to give it a warm glow.

If you find the windows are still lacking, you may want to create additional geometry, like trim and a window frame. This will help you add realism to the scene and can also make your shadows more interesting. Every detail helps!

Render settings

Modifying render settings is one of the simplest tasks in 3D animation, but has the greatest effect on your final output. Click on the **Render Settings** icon (third in the render icons palette) to get started. The following is a screenshot of the **Render Settings** window:

The **Output** tab contains all the information you'll need if you plan to save images to your computer. So far we've only rendered temporary images that are gone as soon as you click on the window, but if you plan to export an animation (as we will in the next chapter) or need to save out still images, this is where you'll start. The default image size is 800 x 600 pixels. Here, you can change the aspect ratio of your images, their final output size, as well as how many frames to render out of your timeline for an animation. We won't export any images until the next chapter, but for now, experiment with changing your size to see how this affects the camera's field of view. Changing the width and height to 1280 x 720 (a standard 720p HD output) changes the field of view dramatically—you can adjust the camera position to overcompensate if you wish. We'll be animating our camera in the next chapter.

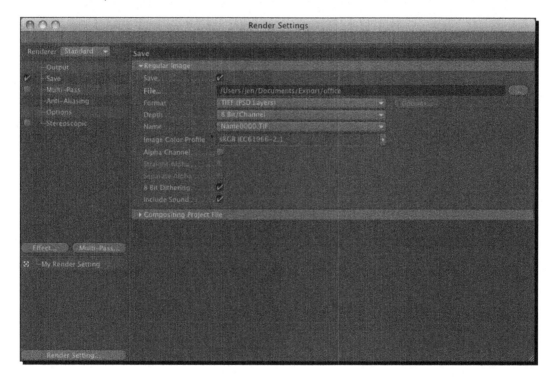

The **Save** tab works hand-in-hand with the **Output** tab, allowing you to specify a location to save your files, as well as file type and additional compositing options.

We will discuss the **Multi-Pass** tab in *Chapter 10, Optimizing Your Workflow*. This allows you to export individual channels for compositing, allowing for easier adjustments in post-production. For example, if you worry that your shadows may be too intense (or too subtle), but you're concerned about long render times, exporting a separate "shadow pass" will allow you to add on shadows and control their appearance as a separate layer in external software such as Adobe After Effects or Adobe Photoshop, without spending twice the render time. This is a very useful tool that we'll explore in greater detail after we've created our animation.

Under the **Anti-Aliasing** tab, make sure your settings are turned to **Best**. The default levels (**1 x 1** and **4 x 4**) strike an acceptable balance between quality and render time for most scenes. Increasing these levels will result in longer render times, but will also yield cleaner renders. It's easiest to notice the difference in anti-aliasing values when you pay attention to areas of your scene with straight lines. If you notice a stairstep effect or anything that looks a little jittery, try increasing the value of your minimum and maximum levels before attempting to overcompensate in the geometry or texture of an object.

The **Options** tab contains basic settings that can be turned on and off, such as allowing transparency, reflection, and shadow. These should always be enabled and controlled via materials, however, if you need to export a quick test render, this is an easy way to disable some of the features of materials that will increase render time. They will greatly impact the look of your final render, but this is an easy global way to disable certain settings in specific cases.

The **Stereoscopic** tab will aid you if you are creating a stereoscopic (anaglyph or polarized) animation where the viewer will be wearing special glasses to interpret overlapping images.

The **Effect...** button opens up a secondary menu with a number of additional render options. Many of these will apply post effects (such as **Glow** and **Depth of Field**), but some of them can be very helpful as we consider how to light our scene.

Select **Ambient Occlusion** from the top of the list. Leave all the settings at default for now and perform a test render to get a screenshot similar to the following one:

Ambient Occlusion is a quick way to reinforce edges and intersections of your objects, darkening the shadows toward intersections in order to create a more extreme contrast. While it does increase render time, it is often thought of as a quicker alternative to **Global Illumination**. Uncheck the **Ambient Occlusion** box, click on the **Effect** button and select **Global Illumination**, and then perform a test render. Leave the settings at default for now:

Let's compare our standard render against our render with **Ambient Occlusion** and **Global Illumination**:

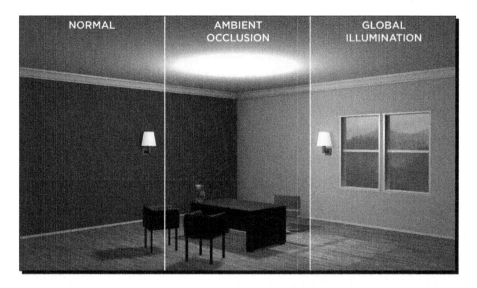

As you can see, color and shadow are highly affected by adding effects. It's best to not think of these things as additional options to tack on at the end, but to work with them from the very beginning as you light and texture a scene. Deciding your render settings from the beginning has multiple advantages, as follows:

◆ It allows you to better control render time. You see render time increase gradually rather than being surprised when you "tack on" an effect at the end.

◆ It allows for easier control over materials and lighting. You see how everything works together as you go rather than having to constantly re-adjust as you alter render settings.

◆ It allows you to save time on modeling potentially unnecessary details that would be lost due to lighting, material, and rendering decisions.

At this point, you should decide what is best for your renders based on the computer you're using and the look you wish to achieve. Since we will be animating this scene soon, it will be useful to look at your frame render time. While a 3-minute render time may be appropriate for an attractive still image, a 30-second animation at 30 frames per second will require you to export 900 individual images—meaning your final render time will be 2700 minutes. For now, you may want to keep settings relatively low as we continue working.

Moving forward, the test renders shown here will use both **Global Illumination** and **Ambient Occlusion** to show our lighting in the best possible conditions. We will learn additional optimization tips and tricks along the way that will be helpful if you choose to use lower quality render settings.

Time for action – placing accurate lighting

So far we've examined the properties of lights through just one global room light, but now let's create a more detailed look by adding additional lights to the scene.

1. First, let's create small lights for our wall lamps. Create an **Omni** light with an **Intensity** of **50%** and a color of (**255**, **230**, **180**). Give it a falloff of 80 cm, and set the shadows to soft. Place this Omni light inside of the lampshade (a quick way to do this is to set the omni as a child of the lampshade, then change its Object Rel coordinates to (0, 0, 0), this will move the child to the exact location of the parent's axis). Then, create an instance of the light (so that the settings are identical if you choose to change the light temperature, falloff, and so on later on) and place it in the other lampshade:

2. So far, we've had just one light illuminating our room. For this scene, we want a softer, less pointed look; we don't have a ceiling fixture, so we just want general illumination for the room. Instead of using a single Omni light with full brightness, we're going to use four overlapping lights with less brightness.

3. Change the settings of our current light to a brightness of 35 percent, with a falloff of 300 cm. Leave the shadow values as they are. Move the light to (-125 cm, 200 cm, 125 cm). Then, create three copies of the light, placing them at (225 cm, 200 cm, 125 cm), (-125 cm, 200 cm, -225 cm), and (225 cm, 200 cm, -225 cm). The color of the lights have been changed for the view below to make them show better in your **Top** view, however, this image is a good guide to check your placement:

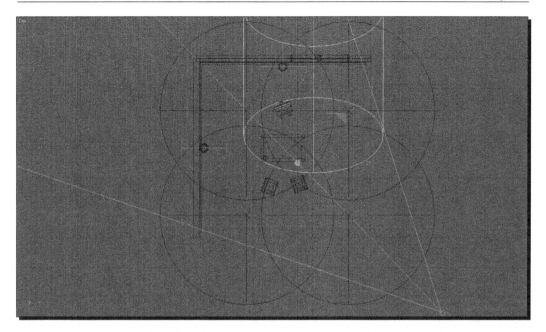

4. The lighting in our room should now appear much more global and less pointed than the lighting obtained in the previous render of our office model. However, now that we have four lights, we still have a serious problem of how their presence affects the ceiling, as shown in the following new screenshot:

5. Let's employ a technique to light the ceiling as an individual object and have it be unaffected by the additional lights in the scene. We discussed previously that sometimes emulating real-world conditions means you end up "faking" those conditions through some interesting tricks, this is one of them! Create a new Omni light. Name it **Ceiling Light** so you don't mix it up with your other global lights. Click on the **Project** tab; make sure the drop-down next to **Mode** says **Include**, then drag-and-drop the Ceiling object into the empty box below.

6. For the four global lights, we'll follow a similar process. Select all four of them (or the main Omni if you're using instances instead of live copies), navigate to **Project**, make sure **Mode** is set to **Exclude**, and drag-and-drop the **Ceiling** object into the empty box. Set the ceiling light to 60 percent brightness, and then perform a test render.

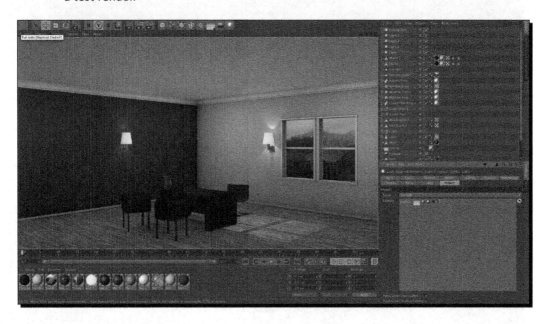

What just happened?

We've emulated real-world lighting conditions through a combination of real lighting (putting lights inside of our lampshades) and some visual tricks (creating a lighting grid and setting up a separate light exclusively for the ceiling). As you create more scenes and progress in your lighting technique, it's important to constantly evaluate if your scene is behaving as it should. Placing lights in the locations that are perfectly accurate from a technical standpoint means nothing in the scene looks wrong!

We've discussed before that 3D isn't a perfectly linear process. Modeling, texturing, and lighting often overlap to a great degree. Lighting alone is far from linear, but it's good to follow this general process:

1. Establish a global lighting plan.
2. Add object-specific lighting (in our case, lamps).
3. Adjust specific areas as necessary (adding lights or changing brightness in darker areas; isolating specific elements if necessary).

Regardless of the type of scene you're working on—interior, object, or abstract—this process works well across the board.

Pop quiz – lighting and rendering basics

We've wrapped up our lighting plan for the scene, but let's make sure we've got the concepts down as we progress into animation.

Q1. In order to ensure consistency, which render settings should be considered when setting up a scene?

Q2. What are the basic types of lights, and how are they created?

Q3. One specific object in a scene appears too blown out, but nearby objects all look as they should. What are the two possible solutions?

Summary

Congratulations! You've made it! We have a fully textured, fully lit, realistic model. Our animation in the next chapter will consist of animating a camera around this room. Our render settings may change slightly, and we may find that our lighting changes a little when we look from a different angle, but we've got a very solid beginning that will lead to beautiful animation soon. We're well on our way to mastering the following concepts:

- Types of lights and how they are best used
- Basic light settings and how to avoid lighting that is "too much" in terms of highlights and shadows
- Global render settings and how they will affect our render times
- Adding realism through simple steps such as projecting an image on a plane and shining sunlight through a window

Chapter 6, Animation, will give us a whole new dimension to think about: time! Make sure you love how your office looks now, because we'll be moving all around it soon!

6
Animation

Now that we've created a fully textured and lit office model, let's learn how to create an animation that shows it off. We'll briefly discuss timeline-based animation, then move into setting up and editing keyframes. This chapter will discuss the comparative benefits of auto-keying versus manually creating keyframes, editing keyframes, and how to optimize your render for final output. We'll animate a camera, explore ways to animate the buttons on our cell phone, and discuss animated materials.

In this chapter we will learn about:

◆ Linear animation

◆ Animatable properties for different types of objects

◆ Camera animation

◆ Keyframing

◆ Curve editing

◆ Additional render requirements for animation

Before we begin

Over the next three chapters, we'll spend most of our time understanding how to make things move. Each chapter will focus on a specific set of principles:

◆ *Chapter 6, Animation*, introduces linear animation, keyframing, and basic animation within Cinema 4D

◆ *Chapter 7, MoGraph*, introduces a procedural approach to animation used for motion graphics

◆ *Chapter 8, XPresso*, introduces a node-based programming language that facilitates procedural animation by connecting individual objects and setting up linked behaviors

Chapter 7, MoGraph and *Chapter 8, XPresso* will detail animation methods to build on the basic motion principles we learn in this chapter. Let's get started!

Animation – key terms and how it works

So far, we've created our model through the eye of a still lens—a composition that is static. Animation can be thought of in a number of different ways, but it is ultimately a series of still images displayed rapidly so your eye is tricked into seeing those still images as one continuous, dynamic composition. The number of images (known in animation as frames) per second depends on how they will be presented—filmmakers work in 24 frames per second (or fps), while some animators work at 30 fps for web and other media. If an animation looks "choppy", this is mostly likely due to a low frame rate, and if something looks overly sharp, it may be due to a very high frame rate. There are often deliberate reasons behind using a different frame rate, such as stop-motion animation that works at a much lower frame rate to achieve a jittery output, but for the most part you will want to set up your compositions in either 24 or 30 fps. If you are familiar with drop-frame rates such as 29.97 or 23.976, be aware that C4D renders whole frames. You will want to handle the conversion in post-production with an appropriate method for your final output.

Early animations were created by hand, by drawing individual images, placing them in order and cycling from image to image very quickly. Computer-generated animation has made two basic approaches possible—**Linear animation** and **Non-linear animation**. Non-linear animation is a type of animation that focuses on the actions of objects in a scene without being bound to a specific amount of time, while linear animation is created in a timeline.

Linear animation is generated through the use of keyframes. In traditional animation, a senior animator would be responsible for drawing the beginning and ending points for objects in motion, and a more junior assistant would create the "inbetweens". In computer-generated animation, the software will function as your assistant! If an object needs to move in a straight line from point A to point B—say, from (0 cm, 0 cm, 0 cm) to (0 cm, 0 cm, 200 cm), two keyframes will be sufficient. If the object needs to behave in a different way—perhaps arcing in the center to (0 cm, 100 cm, 100 cm), a third keyframe can be added in the middle to help guide the object to the behavior you desire (the behavior between two keyframes can also be controlled using Bezier curves on a timeline).

Time for action – timeline animation

The tools we've learned so far have all been accessed through default palettes in the **Startup Layout**. For animation, we need an additional palette, the **Timeline**. You can navigate to the timeline in two different ways: by changing your layout to the Animation layout (**Window | Customization | Layouts | Animation**), or, if you've customized your layout and don't want to lose the way you've moved things, you can simply navigate to **Window | Timeline** and open the timeline in a new, detached palette, or you can change your layout to the Animation layout (**Window | Customization | Layouts | Animation**), as shown in the following screenshot:

Depending on which layout option you choose, your timeline may look slightly different than the following one, which shows the detached **Timeline** window. Remember that you can dock the timeline in any location on your custom layout by clicking-and-dragging the grid icon at the top-left side, as shown in the following screenshot:

Let's add a couple of keyframes and explore our timeline!

1. Select the **Camera** object in the Objects Manager. Make sure the camera you've selected is the camera you're currently looking through. The icon to the right of the object should be white instead of gray, as shown in the following screenshot:

2. Underneath the viewport, you'll see an abridged version of the timeline, as well as a row of icons that we'll use for keyframing, as shown in the following screenshot. Make sure the green marker is set at zero. Look for the green vertical rectangle which should be all the way to the left of the timeline. You can also look to the right of the timeline, which should say **0 F**, indicating that the marker is currently at frame 0. You can always navigate to different points in the timeline by either dragging the marker in the timeline under the viewport or in your separate **Timeline** window, manually enter a frame number, or move one frame forward or backward using the *F* and *G* keys on your keyboard. Click on the icon that looks like a pink circle with a key on it—this will create a keyframe at frame 0:

3. Take a look at your **Timeline** window. You should now see your **Camera** object, with a blue rectangle next to it representing a keyframe. If you see all of your objects in your timeline, navigate to **View | Show | Show Animated**. Many animators find it helpful to right-click on the desired object in the Objects Manager, then select **Show Tracks**. You can easily switch between these modes and you will most likely find that one of them suits your working style better than the other. For our purposes, we'll keep the animated objects isolated to keep our timeline simple, as shown in the following screenshot:

4. As you can see, we have keyframes for **Position**, **Scale**, and **Rotation**. However, for animating our camera, we only need position and rotation data—scale won't help us much here! Look at the row of icons where we originally created the keyframe and click on the **Scale** icon (the center icon in the position/scale/rotation set) to deactivate it, as shown in the following screenshot. This ensures that future keyframes, which we create will only be **Position** and **Rotation**:

5. Let's create a 10 second camera animation of our environment. First, make sure that your project settings are at 30 fps by navigating to **Edit | Project Settings**. In the Attributes Manager, set **FPS** to **30** and **Maximum Time** to **300 F**, as shown in the following screenshot:

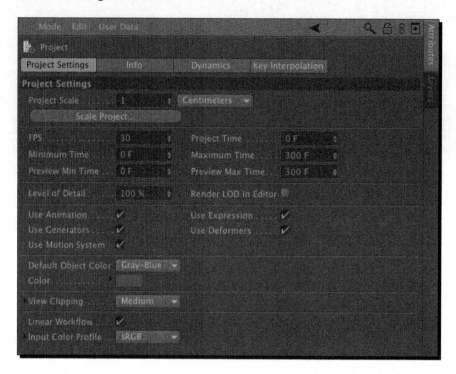

6. Move the marker to **300 F** on your timeline. Click on the middle icon of the keyframing icons, next to the icon we used to create our first keyframe. This enables **Automatic Keyframing**. We'll discuss the benefits and drawbacks of auto-keying soon, but for now, let's use it to help us create our ending keyframe of the animation. You can either re-position the camera through the viewport (using the regular viewport navigation controls) or move the camera object itself. If you choose the second method, make sure you leave the **Perspective** viewport window open, so you can double-check the new ending composition. Since we originally created only two walls for the room, you may need to add additional geometry to your scene, as shown in the following screenshot:

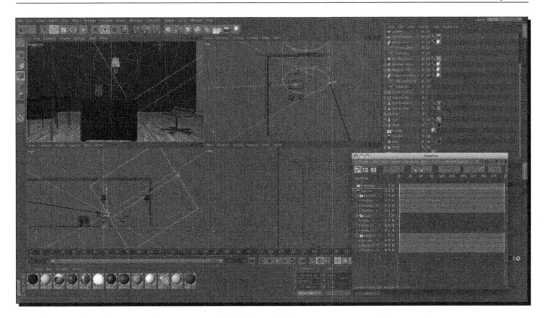

What just happened?

We've learned two ways to create keyframes, as well as how to control which properties we're animating and how to define our project settings.

There are a few things to keep in mind as you animate:

- Before you create a new keyframe, make sure you've specified the parameters for animation. Keyframed parameters can, and usually do, operate independently of one another. So, say you're animating your camera over 150 frames from (0 cm, 200 cm, 0 cm) to (200 cm, 200 cm, 200 cm), but want it to dip down to (100 cm, 0 cm, 100 cm) in the middle. However, you want the camera to rotate smoothly from 0 to 90 degrees over the entire 150 frame animation, which only requires two keyframes. Your best course of action would be to key the rotation and position at frames 0 and 150, then deactivate the rotation option and add a position-only keyframe at 75. As a general rule, the fewer the keyframes you can place, the better—it allows for smoother, more easily customizable animation.

◆ Auto-keying can be a quick and easy way to create animation on the fly. It's a very handy approach to beginning keyframes, particularly when it comes to camera animation—scroll through the timeline, place keyframes, and then refine them on the timeline afterward. However, make sure you keep a constant eye on which objects you have selected, and also routinely check your timeline to ensure you haven't accidentally keyed something else. Remember that auto-keying will only create keyframes for the properties you have active, so if you move an object and rotate it but only have position selected, you'll miss half of your properties. The reverse holds true as well—if you have all the options activated, you will create new position, rotation, and scale keyframes every time you make a change.

◆ Auto-keying will also apply to every object in a scene. So, if you're working on a camera animation, and you realize that an object's rotation or position doesn't really work when you've moved the camera to a new spot, changing anything about the object will now be keyframed. So, if you're at frame 75 and want to move your object, and then realize at frame 150 that it should be somewhere else, the object will animate from frames 75 to 150—probably not what you want! Auto-keying can be a great tool, but it's important to remember that every new parameter you define is being recorded as an animated setting and not as a global one.

Animatable properties

So far, we've discussed animation in terms of position, scale, and rotation. One of the strengths of Cinema 4D is that almost any property of an object can be animated! Select any object in your scene—we'll use our outdoor sunlight as an example—and let's examine its properties from an animation perspective.

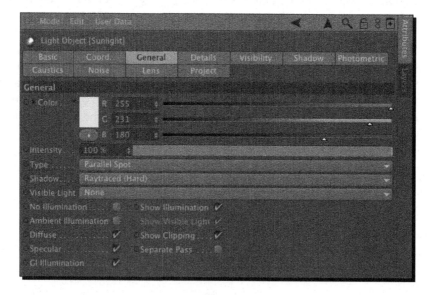

The open circles to the left of all the properties shown in the preceding screenshot represent an animatable property. This means you can animate **Color** and **Intensity** of the light over time, as well as change **Type** and turn off and on various checkboxes.

On attributes that are a simple on or off state, it is usually best to key a different attribute, if possible. Since there is no numeric to change, that is a gradual shift from 0 to 100 percent intensity, this will result in an immediate total change. If you want to change one of these fundamental properties, such as changing from a soft to hard shadow, you may also want to overcompensate by adjusting the color or density of your shadows as well.

To create a keyframe, hold down the *command* key and left-click on the circle next to the property you want to animate. When the open outlined circle changes to a red solid circle, it indicates a keyframe has been successfully created, as shown in the following screenshot:

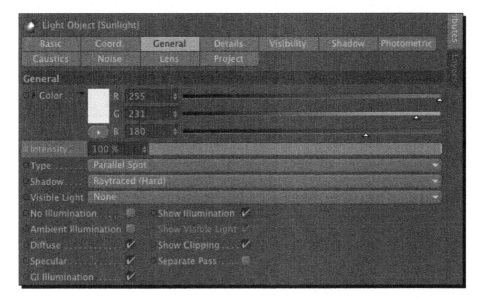

If you change the value of a keyed property and do not have auto-keying turned on, the icon will turn yellow, as shown in the next screenshot. This means that an attribute has been modified, but the change will not actually take place until you press *command* along with clicking on the icon again. If you do not place a keyframe, it will change back to its original value as soon as you move the marker in the timeline.

If auto-keying is turned on, the property will auto-key as long as one other keyframe already exists. The property has to be activated similarly to the position/rotation/scale options under the viewport. Otherwise, this will create a global change.

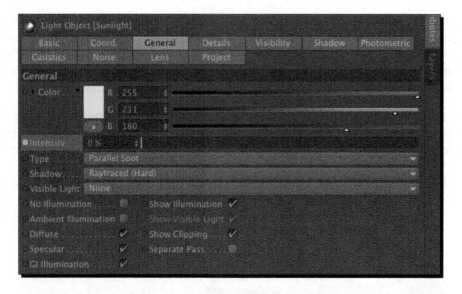

Have a go hero – animated lights

Using the additional style of keyframing we just learned, we're going to animate the lights turning on in our scene. Keep a couple of things in mind:

- Create a keyframe by pressing *command* along with clicking on the open circle to the left of the property you want to animate. Make sure the circle turns to red before you move the marker in the timeline.

- Auto-keying will apply only to those properties for which you have already created at least one keyframe.

- If you have materials that use the Luminance channel, you will need to key their brightness as well, provided that you choose to animate all of the lights in the scene. If you don't animate all lights (that is, if you choose to only change the sunlight and leave the rest of the room constant), then you may or may not need to animate luminance.

- Anything can be keyed at any time, so if you want to add style by offsetting the timing, this can achieve a very realistic and visually compelling look.

The following screenshots show a sample staggered timeline for animated objects and materials, followed by five sample frames: 60, 120, 180, 240, and 300 (with all the lights at 0 percent, the scene in frame 0 appears completely black):

At frame 120, we begin to see some color in our room, as well as some dim illumination on our furniture and wall décor:

In frame 180, our wall sconces are becoming brighter and we get a better balance between the harsh light from outdoors and what we see inside:

For our final two frames, our lighting gradually ramps up to its full, final state. Our final frame shows just a hint of the harsh light from outdoors, and we can now fully focus on all of our objects in the scene:

Our final two keyframes at 240 (the previous screenshot) and 300 (the following screenshot) show a subtle shift as our camera's position and rotation eases into its final resting state and our lights all reach their final intensity:

The following timeline shows where all the aforementioned keyframes are placed, for your reference:

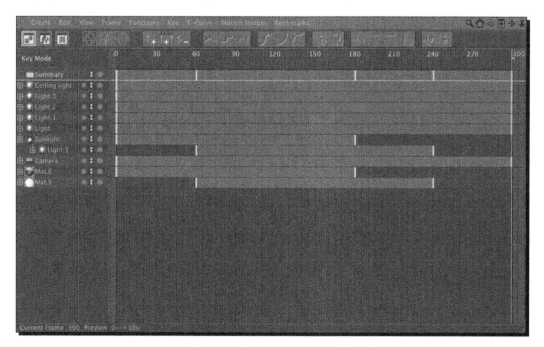

How to plan your animation

In a perfect world, we would be able to plan out every single detail of an animation before we began, following step-by-step instructions the whole way. In the real world, that just doesn't happen! All sorts of things can change as you move through an animation—the script changes, or you record new audio that moves faster, or the final file is now going to be displayed on a television instead of a website. We rarely have the opportunity to control every variable, but there are a set of guidelines we can follow to keep things running as (relatively) smoothly as possible!

◆ Before you begin, think about the type of animation you want to create. Think about your audience, and the message you want to convey. If you're creating an architectural animation of a store, do you want to see every single piece of the puzzle, or is it safe to only focus on one or two key areas? Is there enough content there to keep the viewer engaged for three minutes as we slowly wind through the environment, or would this best be shown quickly with a fast camera pushing through the scene? If you're working on a motion graphics piece, is the tone slow and ethereal or exciting and fast? Often, these questions are very easy to answer; think about your audience and consider the client's brand or the feeling you want to evoke from your viewers. Professional animators rely heavily on storyboards as a way to pre-visualize a project from start to finish, as well as communicate ideas to clients. If you are working in a team, storyboards are helpful to make sure everyone is working together and knows the common end goal.

◆ If your animation has a soundtrack, consider at least putting together a rough version of your audio track with music and voiceover if desired. Putting together your audio will help you understand the feeling you're trying to convey, and that can aid you in pacing along the way. Cinema 4D offers audio playback options within the timeline. Note that as your scenes become more complex, real-time animation playback may not be possible.

◆ Cinema 4D creates keyframes that are eased by default. If you expand your timeline, you'll notice that the lines between keyframes are not straight, but have Bezier handles, as shown in the following screenshot. This means that the animation of an object will be slower as it approaches and moves away from keyframes, and will be fastest right in the middle. The easing between keyframes can be defined by adjusting the Bezier handles to create your ideal timing, or by right-clicking on a keyframe and choosing a new mode. Experiment with various types and watch how their interpolation changes. You can also make adjustments to keyframes by selecting them and looking at your options in the Attributes Manager.

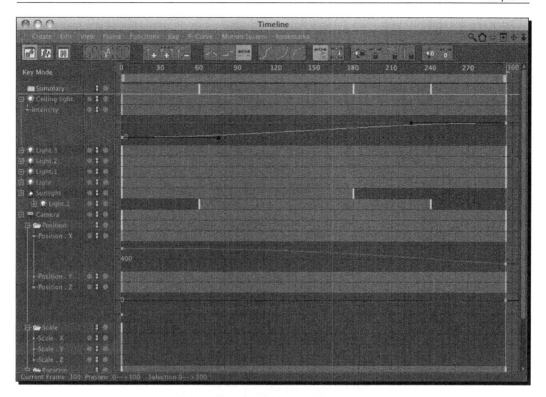

- ◆ Since most keyframes in Cinema 4D will be eased and controlled by their curves, it is ideal to use as few keyframes as possible. As a general rule, animation is smoother—and much easier to control—with fewer keyframes. As you plan out your animation, try to think as high-level as you possibly can, planning out the motion through an entire scene rather than placing one keyframe. If you need to define five specific keyframes, rather than going 1-2-3-4-5-, it is common practice to place 1-5-3 followed by 2 and 4 as necessary. You will most likely find that you need far fewer keyframes if you start with the beginning and ending and then make modifications by dividing up sections of your animation as evenly as possible.

- ◆ The size of a render can be changed at any time, but it's best to at least begin with your renders set up to the correct aspect ratio. Most animations are created at a 16:9 aspect ratio, regardless of their output. With online video sites such as YouTube and Vimeo allowing HD content, and computer monitors shifting toward widescreen as opposed to the standard 4:3 aspect ratio, HD content is becoming the general standard. If necessary, HD content can be "letterboxed" and shrunk to fit the 4 x 3 aspect ratio horizontally, with black bars at the top and bottom to fill the extra space. It's always safe to try and find out your final output from the beginning, though, because this will affect your compositional framing as you create cameras. Be sure to ask clients early on, or if you can decide the final output on your own, consider the delivery method.

Render settings

Now that we've set our keyframes and worked on our motion paths, we should see how the whole piece flows together. Depending on the speed of your computer and the complexity of your scene, you may simply be able to hit play and see a draft rendering. Keep in mind, though, that this may be playing much slower than intended; the computer will play through as quickly as possible, which will most likely not be at 30 fps. At this point you can either create a preview render, or you can create a full render—what you do is up to you and depends on how much available time you have for your renders. You can turn render settings down; turning off ambient occlusion and global illumination are easy fixes, but there is also a better way if you're just looking to preview the animation path. Preview Rendering allows you to export a low-resolution Quicktime file. Click and hold on the **Render to Picture Viewer** icon to expand the options, as shown in the following screenshot:

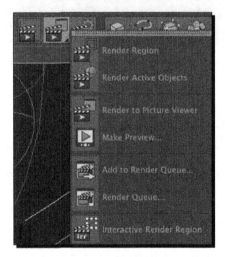

Then select **Make Preview**:

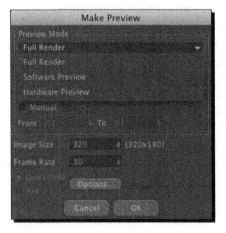

Clicking on **Full Render** will expand the options for rendering. **Hardware Preview** is an excellent low-res option for checking animation, because it will export an animation that looks identical to the preview you're used to seeing in your viewport. However, rendering as a **Full Render** is a valuable option for checking small sections—that is if you want to see a 1 second clip when one of the lights finishes where textural animation is involved. The **Image Size** determines the width of an image; the height is automatically generated depending on the aspect ratio you've set in your Render Settings.

Clicking on **Options** will allow you to change how the final file is compressed. The Animation codec (Cinema's default setting) will result in a Quicktime movie that is a very large size, but is one of the lowest possible levels of compression. Your compression options may differ based on which codecs are installed on your computer natively, as well as other video and animation software you may have installed. H.264 is a common standard for well-compressed animation. If you are just doing a preview render, which you presumably won't keep, file size may be less of a concern. Larger files will have a harder time with playback than smaller files, however. Software rendering directly to the Picture Viewer is an option that will allow you to decide after rendering if you want to keep the animation. The following is a screenshot of the **Compression Settings** window:

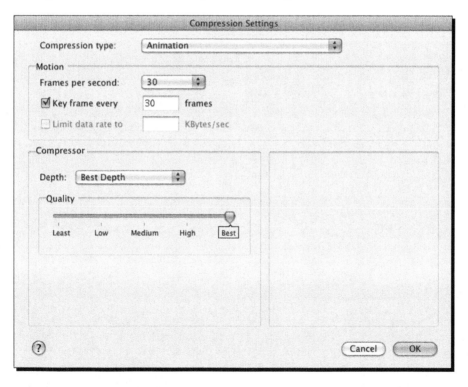

When you click on the **OK** button, a preview render will begin. You can track the progress in the lower-left corner of the screen, which should say **Calculating Preview....** A blue progress bar will appear, as follows:

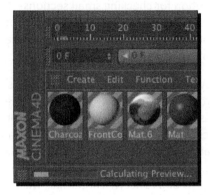

If you are ready to export a full render, there are a number of steps to take. The following screenshots will give you a guide to basic settings, but many of these parameters will be defined by the output you need for your specific file:

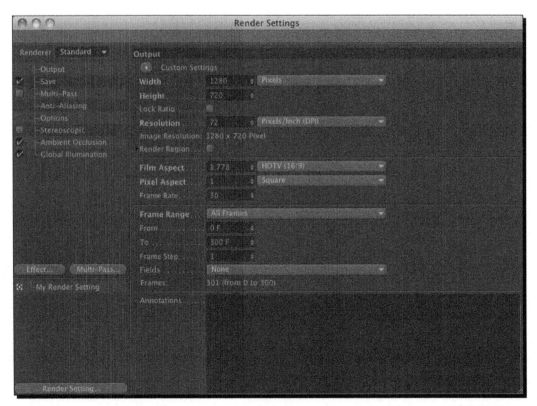

The **Output** tab will let you set the width and height for your images. Most important for animation, though, is the **Frame Range**. You can set it to render just one frame (if you're rendering a still image), all frames (which is dependent on the timeline you defined in your **Project Settings**), or a specific range (if you want to render just a section of the animation):

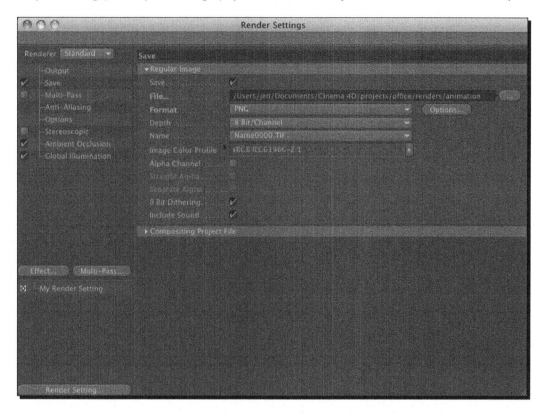

The **Save** tab allows you to specify a location for your files, as well as file type, whether or not to render with an alpha channel (we'll discuss this in a later chapter, but for now leave the box unchecked) and export settings, which we will also discuss later on.

Animations can be exported as a Quicktime file directly, however, it is common practice to export an image sequence instead. This will generate 301 (from 0-300) individual files that you can connect together in Quicktime, After Effects, Final Cut Pro, or a number of third-party tools. There are a number of reasons for this, as follows:

- If you have a long render time (multiple minutes per frame), this method allows you to spot-check individual images as they render, as opposed to waiting for the entire render before being able to analyze frames

- If you find that a section needs to be changed, for example, if frames 60-90 have an error—it is easy to re-render over individual frames, as opposed to rendering out a second Quicktime movie and patching them together

- If your render crashes for any reason, or if there is any sort of corruption in frames, it is easy to re-render specific sections and quickly see which frames rendered successfully

The format you render to is up to you—Targa is a popular option if you need to render with an alpha channel but creates larger files on average, PNG files offer a decent balance of crispness, file size, and so on. Specify a location for your files—remember that there will be as many individual files as there are frames in your sequence, so make sure you don't accidentally render 5400 frames to your desktop! The file path shown previously will create a series of files and save them to the "renders" folder, and they will be named `animation0001.png, animation0002.png,` and so on.

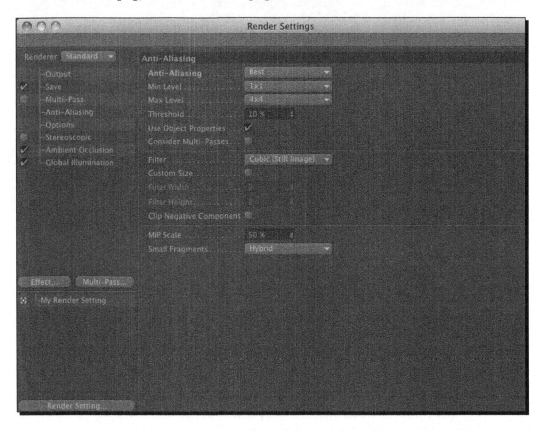

We've discussed **Anti-Aliasing** settings in the previous chapters. However, when it comes to animation, there are a couple of different options to consider. The default **Filter** setting is for **Cubic (Still Image)**. There is an animation setting, as well. The current setting will result in the cleanest image possible, while the animation option creates a slightly softer image. At 30 fps, a series of still images will look very crisp. If you plan to apply any sort of motion blur in post-processing, it may be best to leave the image sequence to still images for versatility. For the most part, you may not notice much of a difference between the two—experiment with multiple methods to see which ones are ideal for your final output:

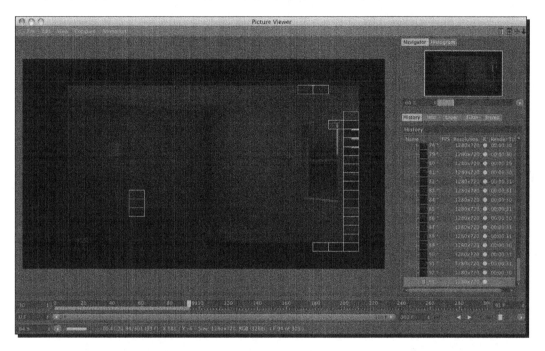

When you have finished creating your render settings, click on the **Render to Picture Viewer** icon. Your Picture Viewer will keep a record of all of your rendered frames and allow you to view your progress. This will allow you to track many things about your progress; you can see what each individual frame looks like, as well as the time it is taking each frame to render. This will give you a good idea of how long the entire scene will take to render. If this estimation is acceptable, let your render continue to run until it finishes—if you need it faster or think you can afford to give a little more time to it, change your settings accordingly.

Summary

We've covered a lot of basic principles of animation in this chapter, which sets us up for the animations we'll continue to create in the next two chapters. The type of keyframing we've done so far is pretty straightforward and literal, but the basic mechanics will continue to help us as we move into more conceptual motion graphics animation.

In this chapter, we covered basic animation concepts such as keyframing, inbetweens, and frames per second, how to work with a linear timeline, how to create keyframes manually and by auto-keying, which parameters are acceptable for animation and how they are animated, things to think through as you begin an animation, how to edit curves and control easing, and which render settings are important for exporting animation.

In the next chapter, we will work with the MoGraph module, which may or may not be installed with your specific version of Cinema 4D. If you do not have this module installed, feel free to skip to *Chapter 8, XPresso*, which works with XPresso, a part of the standard Cinema 4D installation (or read through the process of working with MoGraph objects in case you wish to install it in the future!). Make sure you save your current file after it is rendered, but we'll be creating new models for use in the next chapter.

7
MoGraph

MoGraph is one of Cinema 4D's most popular modules, allowing users to create stunning animations in a couple of easy steps. In discussing the basic MoGraph objects and how they interact, we'll explore motion graphics techniques to give life to your animations.

MoGraph animations are created by creating basic objects and combining them together in unique and interesting ways. We'll learn the basics here and discuss how to set up their interactions, and your creativity will do the rest! In this chapter we will learn about:

◆ Cloner objects
◆ Effectors
◆ Dynamics
◆ Tracer objects
◆ Text objects

Before we begin

Most of the tools we'll be featuring here are only available in the Broadcast and Studio installations of Cinema 4D. If you are using Prime or Visualize, most of this chapter will not apply to you.

As discussed, this chapter will cover the basics of MoGraph objects and introduce a couple of sample animation ideas, but as you continue to learn and grow as an animator, you'll most likely be taken aback at how many possibilities there are! MoGraph allows you to create objects with a basic set of parameters and combine them in endless ways to create unique animations. Let's dive in and start imagining!

Cloner objects

The backbone of MoGraph objects is the cloner object. At its most basic level, it allows you to create multiple clones of an object in your scene. These clones can then be influenced by effectors, which we will discuss shortly. All **MoGraph** objects can be accessed through the MoGraph menu at the top of your screen. Your menu should look like the following screenshot:

Let's open a new scene to explore cloners. Create a sphere, make sure it is selected, then navigate to **MoGraph | Cloner**. You can parent the sphere to the cloner manually, or hold down the *Alt* key while creating the cloner to parent it automatically:

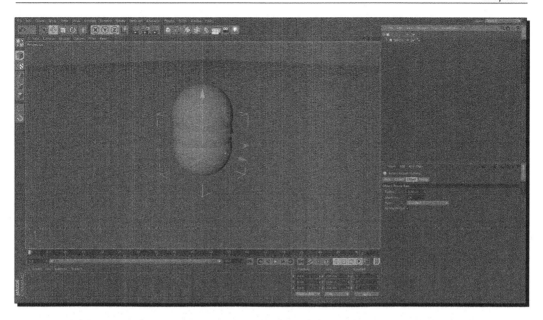

We've cloned our object, but it doesn't look much like clones so far—just a bumpy, vertical pill shape! This is due to the default sizes of our objects not playing well together. Our sphere has a 100 cm radius, and our clones are set 50 cm apart. Let's change the size of our sphere to 25 cm to start. You should now see three distinct spheres stacked on top of each other.

As we create more and more spheres to experiment with cloner settings, you may find that your computer is getting bogged down. We're using a sphere here, but a cube would work just as well and creates far less geometry. You can also reduce your segments on the sphere if desired, but using a simpler form will probably be the most effective method.

Let's take a look at the cloner settings in the Attributes Manager:

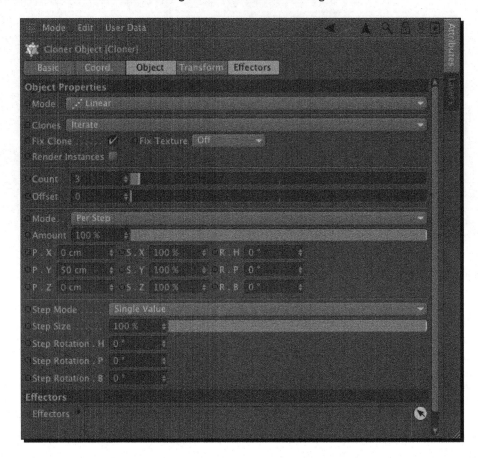

The **Basic** and **Coordinates** tabs follow the same standard as the other object types we've encountered so far, but the **Object** tab is where most of our work will happen.

The first step in using a cloner is to choose a **Mode**:

Object mode arranges clones around any specified additional object in your scene. If you switch your cloner to Object mode, you'll see that you still have an object selected, but the clones have disappeared. This is because the cloner is relying on an object to arrange clones, but we haven't specified one. Try creating any primitive—we'll use a **Capsule** for the following example, then drag it from the Objects Manager into the **Object** field in the Attributes Manager. Since our sphere is relatively large compared to the Capsule, for the moment, let's change its radius to 4 cm. Your objects should be arranged as shown in the following screenshot:

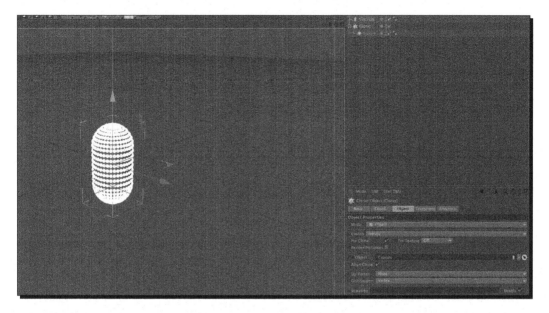

By default, the clones are distributed at each vertex of the object (specified in the **Distribution** field). If you want more or less clones while in Vertex mode, select the capsule and change its height and cap segments accordingly.

Also, the visibility of the clones is linked only to the cloner, and not to the original object. If we turn off visibility on the capsule, the clones stay where they are.

- ◆ **Vertex**: This aligns clones to all vertices (objects can be parametric or polygonal).
- ◆ **Edge**: This aligns clones along edges. Edge will look relatively similar to Vertex but will most likely have significantly more clones. Also this can be used with selection sets to specify which edges should be used.
- ◆ **Polygon Center**: This will look similar to Vertex, but with clones aligned to each polygon. This can be used with selection sets to specify which polygons should be used.
- ◆ **Surface**: This aligns clones randomly to the surface; number of clones is determined by the **count** value.

◆ **Volume**: This fills the object with clones and requires either a transparent material on the original object or turning off visibility:

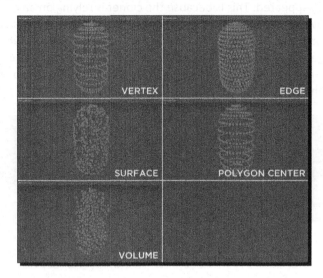

Now that we've explored distribution, let's take a look at the different cloner modes. Linear mode arranges clones in a straight line, while Radial mode arranges clones in a circle—you can think of it as a more advanced version of the Array objects we used when creating our desk chair. Grid Array mode arranges clones in a 3D grid, filling a cube, sphere or cylinder, as shown in the following screenshot. Sounds simple, right? Grid Array, when partnered with effectors, is one of the most powerful tools in your MoGraph toolbox.

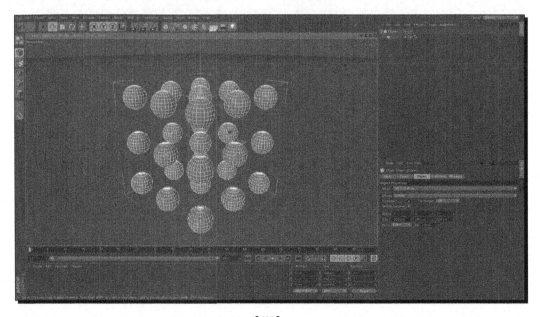

Let's take a look at the settings. The **Count** field allows you to specify how many clones there are in all three directions. The **Size** field will specify the dimensions of the container that the clones fill. This is the key difference from the Duplicate function we learned previously; Duplicate will arrange instances that are spaced *x* distance apart, while the **Size** field on cloners specifies the total distance between the outer-most and inner-most objects. Note that if you change the count of any objects, it adds additional clones inside our cube rather than adding additional rows at the top or bottom, as shown in the following screenshot:

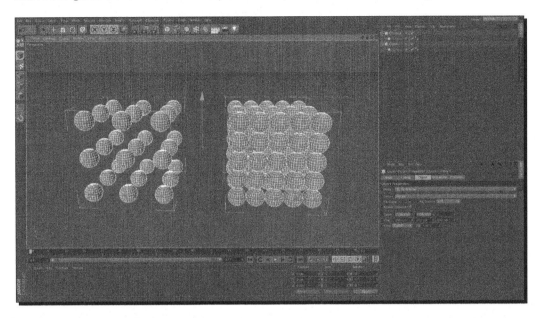

We discussed in earlier chapters that there are often multiple methods of doing things within Cinema 4D, and this is particularly true when it comes to cloners. We used Array objects and the Duplicate function when we were creating our office model, but both of those things could have been easily accomplished using MoGraph as well. Cloners are incredibly versatile, and you may find yourself using them as a modeling tool as you become more comfortable with the software.

Now that we've gotten the basics of cloners down, let's add an Effector and see why this tool is so powerful!

Effectors

Effectors are, very simply, invisible objects in Cinema 4D that influence the behavior of other objects. The easiest way to learn how they work is to dive right in, so let's get started!

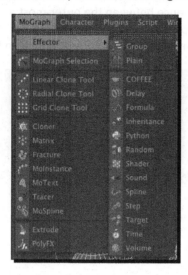

With your cloner object selected (and set back to **Grid Array**, if you've been experimenting with the different modes), navigate to **MoGraph | Effector | Random** as shown in the previous screenshot. You should see all of the clones move in random directions! If you did not select the cloner before creating an effector, they will not be automatically linked. If the clones were unaffected, select the cloner, switch to the **Effectors** tab, and drag the Random effector from the Objects Manager into the open window as shown in the following screenshot:

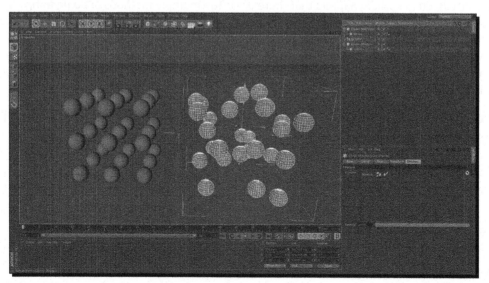

The Random effector is set, by default, to move all objects a maximum of 50 cm in any direction. This takes our clones that exist within the 200 cm cube and allows them to shift an additional 50 cm at random. We're even given an amount of control over that randomness, allowing for endless organic animations.

Let's take a look at the settings for the Random effector:

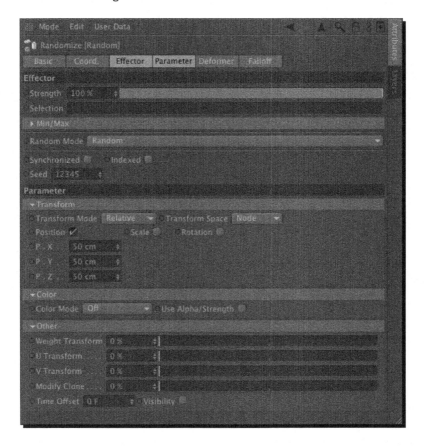

Click-and-drag on the **Strength** slider. As you approach 0 percent, the spheres move closer together. The **Strength** field works directly with the **Transform** parameters, so if you change the strength to 50 percent but leave the Transform values the same, your positions will be identical to a Random effector with 100 percent strength and 25 cm in all directions, as demonstrated in the following screenshot. The cloner on the left is having 50 percent strength, 50 cm x 50 cm x 50 cm, while the cloner on the right is having 100 percent strength, 25 cm x 25 cm x 25 cm:

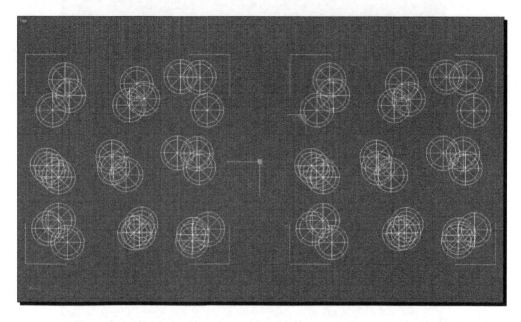

The reason these appear identical is due to their **Seed** value. True randomness is near impossible to create, so random algorithms often rely on a unique number to determine the position of objects. If you change the seed value, it will change the random positions. If you create a Random effector and dislike the result, clicking through seed values until you have a more desirable configuration is a quick and easy way to completely change the scene. This value can be keyframed as well, which can be combined with keyed transformation values to create complicated organic animations very quickly.

In addition to position, you can also randomize scale and rotation. Scale values represent multipliers, rather than a percentage—so a scale of 2 equates to a potential 200 percent increase. 1 is equivalent to 100 percent, meaning a 25 cm sphere may be up to 50 cm—a 100 percent increase. Clicking on the **Uniform Scale** option prevents distorting the sphere.

If you want to test the rotation option and are still using spheres, you may want to create a basic patterned material and add it to your object as shown in the following screenshot - otherwise it'll be impossible to tell that they're rotated!

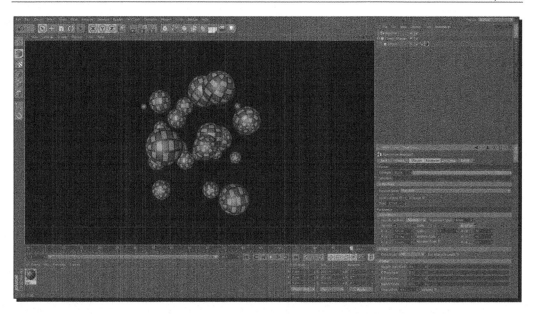

Cloners can have multiple effectors as well. With a cloner selected, navigate to **MoGraph | Effector | Time**. In the Attributes Manager, choose the attributes you'd like to manage over time—perhaps leave the position attributes to the Random effector and add Scale and Rotation to Time—then scroll through the timeline to see how the objects are affected:

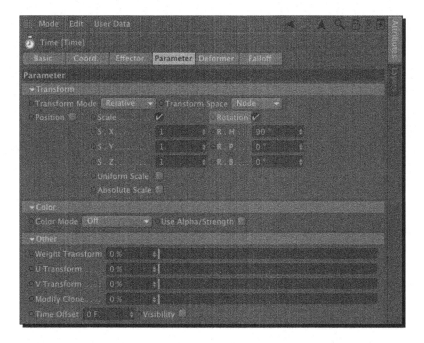

Time for action – creating organic shapes with metaball and cloners

We've used cloners with effectors to change their position, scale, and rotation, but cloners can also be combined with other object types to create interesting effects.

The metaball object allows you to combine individual objects, using the original objects as a guiding shell for a unified single, smooth object.

1. Start a new file, or turn off the other objects in your current scene (which may just be your cloner object at this point).

2. Create three spheres and arrange them spaced slightly apart from one another. Feel free to vary the size as well. The following screenshot shows a 100 cm sphere at (0 cm, 0 cm, 250 cm), a 100 cm sphere at (-185 cm, 0 cm, 0 cm), and a 200 cm sphere at (220 cm, 0 cm, 60 cm):

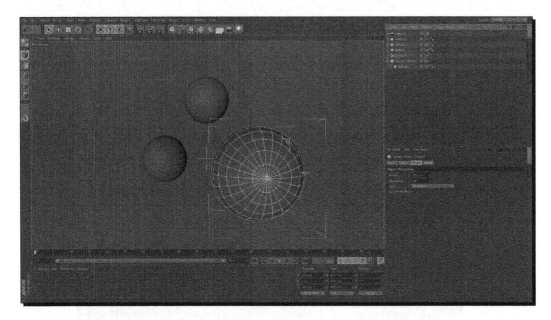

3. Click-and-hold on the Array icon to expand the menu, then click on the **Metaball** object. Parent the three spheres to the metaball. You now have one unified organic shape!

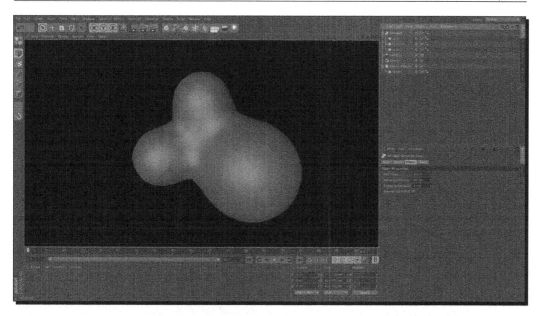

4. Similar to the issues we had when we first created a HyperNURBS object, we now have a model that's a great shape but isn't quite smooth enough. Select the metaball object and change the **Editor Subdivision** and **Render Subdivision** to a much smaller number, 3 cm should do the trick; but if it bogs down your computer down too much, try to find an appropriate balance:

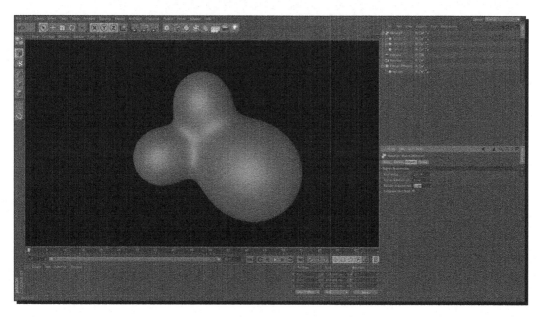

5. Experiment with the metaball object by moving the spheres around and seeing how they interact. Again, if your computer is bogged down, you can change the **Editor Subdivision** to a higher number, then change it back for rendering purposes. Spheres can be pulled away from the rest of the object, but as you move them closer together again, you'll notice the geometry tries to pull and connect. This offers numerous benefits for molecular and other organic styles of animation.

6. Once you've experimented with the three spheres and feel like you have a good handle on how metaball objects work, delete them. Turn your cloner back on, and set it as a child of the metaball object:

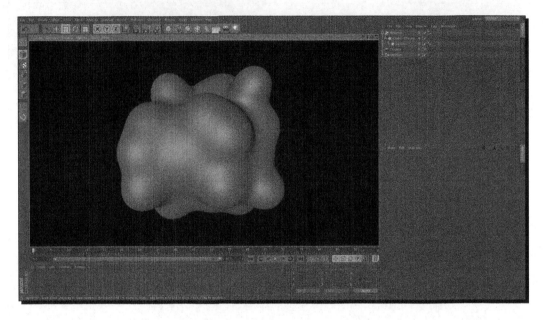

7. From here, you can change the seed in the Random effector to create a different shape, you can change the size of the spheres and add more or less features to them—you now have a basic blob that can be animated however you like!

The frames shown in the next screenshot are from an animation with the following settings:

- A cloner object with a 6 x 1 x 6 count in a 700 x 200 x 250 size
- Keyed metaball position that moves across the screen over 90 frames
- Random effector keyed to change from 12345 to 12348 over 90 frames

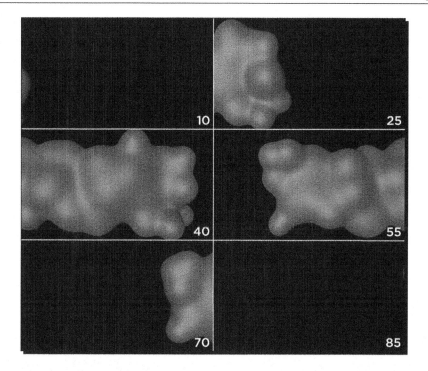

What just happened?

We've discussed along the way that the most powerful solutions in C4D come from taking basic tools and combining them in unique ways. Here, we've combined the metaball object with a MoGraph cloner to create an animated organic form in seconds. There are endless variations on this shape just by modifying the cloner object, useful as the star of the scene or as an ambient background texture.

Now that we've learned how to create a unique, organic animation, let's use our new MoGraph tool to create a more straightforward animation.

Time for action – rigid body tags

There are a number of physics tools built into Cinema 4D, which is one of the many reasons it works so well for motion graphics. Rigid body tags are assigned to objects that will collide with one another through animation, to aid in creating real-world simulations. If you manually animate a ball dropping to a floor, you have to constantly make sure that your object hits the floor at the right position and doesn't accidentally pass through. With dynamics tags, you can ensure that there's no worry!

1. Create a cloner object and change its mode to **Grid Array**. Set its object count at 6 x 1 x 6, and its size to 300 cm x 100 cm x 300 cm. Set a sphere with a 30 cm radius as its child. Then add a Random effector to the cloner. The default transformation setting for position is fine, but let's also enable rotation; 90 degrees on all three directions should work well. Add a texture to your sphere as we did previously so that you can see how the objects are rotating. The following examples will use a basic material with **Tiles** in the **Color** field.

2. Create a **Floor** object. Leave it at (0 cm, 0 cm, 0 cm). Move the cloner object to (0 cm, 600 cm, 0 cm):

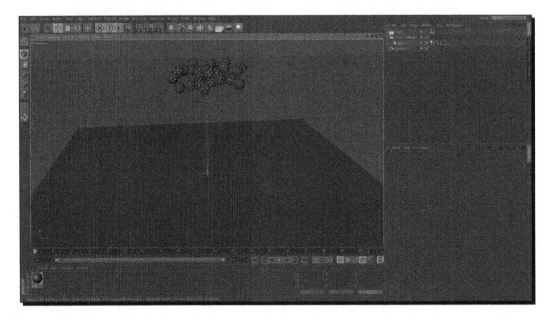

3. Select the **Floor** and the **Sphere** (not the cloner) and, within the Objects Manager, navigate to **Tags | Simulation Tags | Rigid Body**. You should see new tags to the right of your objects as follows:

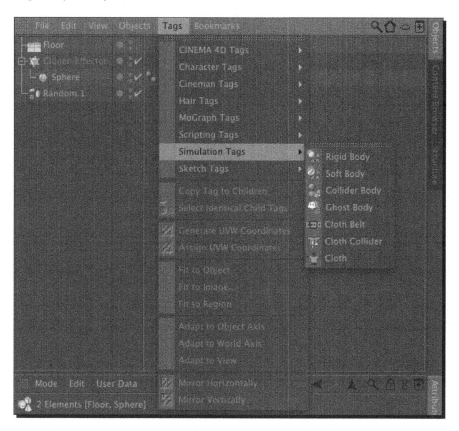

4. Make sure your marker is at frame 0 in your timeline and click on the play button. All the spheres should fall from the sky, hit the floor, and bounce around until they slowly roll to a stop! The following screenshots were rendered with a simple light setup in order to get a sense of space, so these frames may look slightly different than yours. The position and timing, however, should be similar:

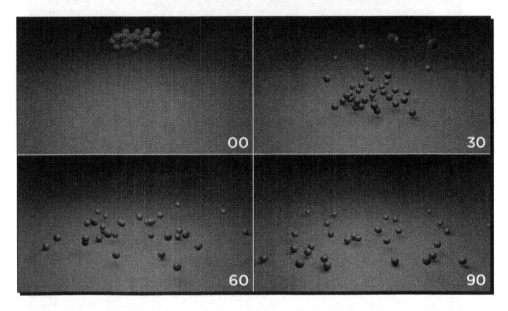

What just happened?

One of C4D's key advantages over the competition is the built-in physics controls, and now we've proven just how simple it is to create realistic animation with a couple of steps.

So how does this animation happen, and how can we control it? If you open your project settings (by navigating to **Edit | Project Settings**) and select the **Dynamics** tab, you'll see some very basic settings. Dynamics are enabled by default, so when you create dynamics tags and haven't specified otherwise, objects will begin moving by default. Experiment with the **Time Scale** and **Gravity** values to see how this affects your scene:

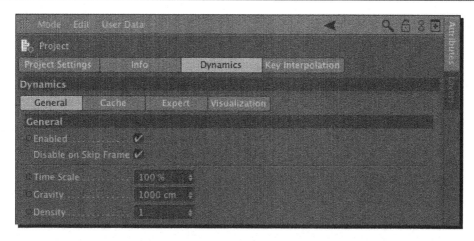

If you need your animation to start at a specific keyframe (rather than frame 0 as in our current animation), the easiest way is to key the **Time Scale**. You can also set keyframes on whether or not dynamics are enabled at all, however, since this is an on-or-off option, keying your Time Scale will allow for a more gradual, natural approach.

There is one very important option on the **Dynamics** tab, Baking. You may have noticed that scrolling through the timeline results in a different look than when you play through the timeline, and if you enter a specific frame value, the viewport may not change at all. Cinema is animating entirely due to dynamics settings and calculating on the fly, rather than creating one motion path that will always remain constant. If you create an animation with dynamics that you're happy with, you can navigate to the **Cache** tab (a subset of the **Dynamics** tab in **Project Settings**) and click on **Bake**, as shown in the following screenshot:

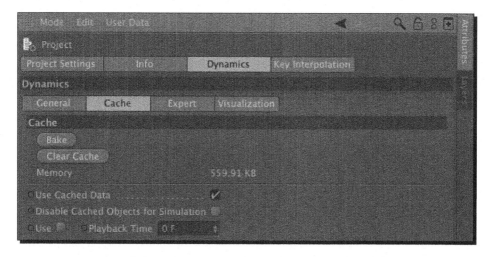

Remember that any changes that are made in the **Project Settings** window are global, applying to everything in your file. Luckily, we're able to set keyframes for individual objects as well. We can enter settings for the floor as well as our individual spheres. If you practiced baking dynamics earlier, re-open the **Project Settings** window and click on **Clear Cache**. Otherwise, the changes we make will not take place, because we just specified that we liked our animation as it was. Additional dynamics settings are located on the Collision tab in the Attributes Manager, as shown in the following screenshot:

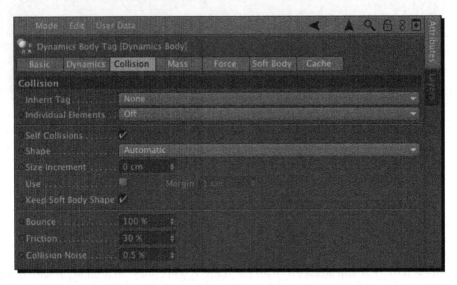

Experiment with changing your **Bounce** value; this is the biggest influencer on the behavior of an individual object. A Bounce value of 0 percent on the sphere's rigid body tag will result in spheres appearing to be stuck to the floor; assigning a Bounce value of 100 percent to the floor will result in very bouncy spheres. Remember that all values can be keyframed, allowing for unlimited variety in your animations.

Have a go hero – MoGraph cloner settings

MoGraph cloner objects and dynamics are incredibly powerful tools with many settings to explore. The best way to explore how these things work is to set up a simple scene like the one we've used previously—a single primitive dropped into a cloner. Click on the play button and see how well your computer handles the number of clones you have in the amount of time you have specified in your timeline (90 frames or 3 seconds, by default).

Keep the frame count low and allow the animation to continue looping. Change a value in the Dynamics settings—bounce, friction, and so on—and watch how your animation immediately responds. This will give you a better understanding of how individual variables can be keyed and combined to create different effects with similar tools. Switch out your primitives as well to see how friction impacts higher-polygon and lower-polygon objects.

MoText objects

If you need to create an extruded type in Cinema, you can create a text spline and place it in an Extrude NURBS object. However, MoGraph has taken one step out of the process with the MoText object! Open the **MoGraph** menu and select **MoText**. This will place an extruded text object in the middle of the stage:

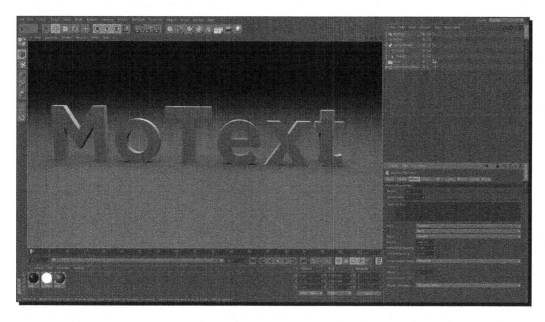

The MoText options in the Attributes Manager are relatively self-explanatory, and all are animatable. Since it is a MoGraph object, it can be used with effectors, as well! Try applying a Step or Random effector and see what the results are! The text itself is keyable as well.

Many of these settings will look very similar to the NURBS and Spline options that we've seen before—Depth, Caps, and so on. MoText is a much more powerful alternative to the text spline, regardless of whether or not animation is your end goal.

Time for action – tracer objects

Motion Graphics designers often find themselves needing to create splines and ribbons that move through space. The tracer object offers a quick and easy way to take the animation path of a spline and create "traced" splines that follow its animation over time.

1. Create a spline—the more points you create, the more processor-heavy your animation will be. The following example will use a standard 4-side spline, 200 cm x 100 cm.

2. Set two keyframes for your spline, using any combination of position/scale/rotation you desire. We'll move our spline from (0 cm, 300 cm, 300 cm) to (0 cm, 300 cm, -300 cm), and rotate on the B axis from 0 to 270 degrees:

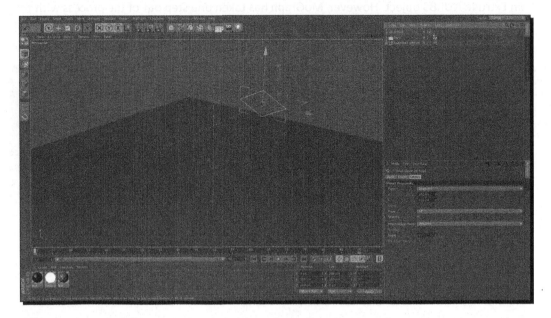

3. With the spline selected, navigate to **MoGraph | Tracer**. Drag your slider through the timeline—if you do not see splines appearing on the screen, select the tracer and make sure the 4-side spline is in the window under **Trace Link**. Drag it into the window if necessary. Your motion paths should be displayed and mapped to the four points of the spline, as shown in the following screenshot:

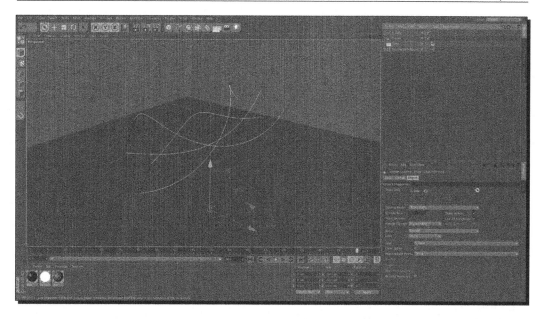

4. Create a Sweep NURBS object, then create a Circle spline. Set the circle's radius to 4 cm. Then, assign the circle and the tracer as children of the Sweep NURBS. Scroll through the timeline and watch your splines grow!

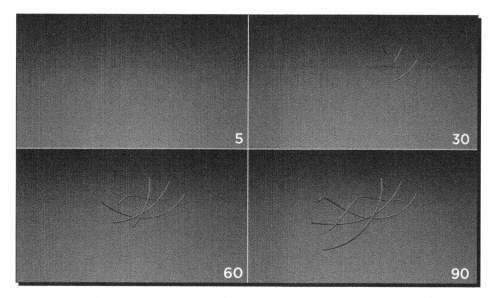

The tracer object is a very powerful tool, but creates very complex geometry. Try and keep your splines as simple as possible, and you'll be on your way to making complex animations in no time!

 If you need your camera to appear as if it is following splines through space, you can parent your animated spline to your animated camera, then trace it. The animation paths will be identical and it will appear as if your camera is "chasing" the spline.

What just happened?

We've used the tracer object to make an object appear to grow! In *Chapter 8, XPresso*, we'll discuss additional ways to link animated properties from one object to another. Each option has its advantages and uses, but for this style of animation, tracer objects are often the easiest way to go. Consider the possibilities of using tracer objects in combination with keying the properties of splines themselves—C4D provides countless ways to create complex, smooth animations.

Summary

We've covered a lot of ground in this chapter, but we've just scratched the surface of MoGraph's capabilities. As MoGraph has developed over the last few versions of Cinema 4D, many generous animators have taken the time to figure out possible combinations of elements and shared them online—Greyscalegorilla, HelloLuxx, and Maxon's own Cineversity are great places to jumpstart your imagination.

In this chapter we've learned how to create cloner objects, how effectors interact with MoGraph objects, how to combine cloners with Cinema's built-in dynamics system to create complex animations by defining simple behaviors, how to create and edit text objects, and how to use tracer objects with simple splines to guide other objects in a scene.

The next chapter explores a node-based programming language that allows you to dynamically link properties from one object to another. It will be slightly more structured than this chapter, leading to one large complex animation at the end. We'll create some very basic models to work with as well, so you may want to brush up on your modeling principles ahead of time.

8
XPresso

XPresso is a node-based programming language that allows you to dynamically link object properties. Whether it's a clock grinding its gears as time passes, a car driving down the street, an expanding pie chart, or doors opening as a camera approaches them, XPresso provides a quick and easy way to produce complex animations.

In this chapter we will learn about:

- ◆ Node-based programming
- ◆ The Expressions editor
- ◆ Linking properties and parameters through XPresso
- ◆ Creating user-defined sliders

Node-based programming

Most programming languages are text-based, that is, they execute commands entirely through expressions written in plain text. These languages have a certain syntax—a set of words, numbers, and punctuation that deliver instructions to a computer on how to perform a task.

Node-based programming languages, however, are a visual alternative. Objects and commands are organized in a visual hierarchy that shows the flow of input and output, allowing you to see how things interact. Node-based programming languages are often easier for first-time programmers to understand, as objects and commands can usually be organized in any visual configuration that makes sense to the programmer without affecting how the program functions.

XPresso is an example of this type of programming, and is the primary language used in Cinema 4D. Many beginner users find XPresso intimidating, but creating basic functions is simple and can save you a lot of time! Let's dig in and see how it works.

Time for action – linking properties with Set Driver and Set Driven

One of the main strengths of XPresso is a simple, straight-forward approach to linking properties between multiple objects. We've used instances and cloners in the past to duplicate objects in order to be able to modify them as a group, but XPresso gives us the unique ability to change individual properties in dissimilar objects. In the following exercise, we'll explore the concept of setting objects as "drivers" and "driven" - linking the properties of one object (the driver) in a way that changes the properties of the others (the driven).

1. Create a cube and make it editable.

2. Create a sphere and make it editable.

3. Move both objects so that they have some space between them; we'll be editing their scale and don't want them to intersect.

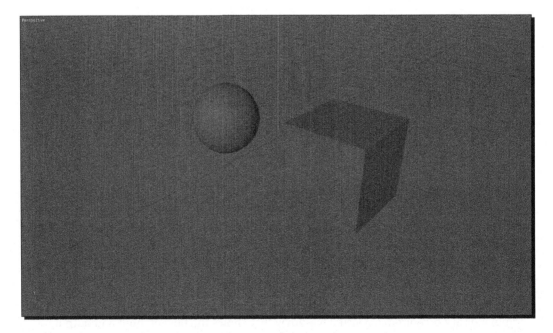

4. Select the cube and right-click on **S. Y** (the Y scale value, but to the left of the input field). On the pop-up menu, select **Animation | Set Driver**. This specifies that we will be using the Y scale of our cube to control properties of other objects.

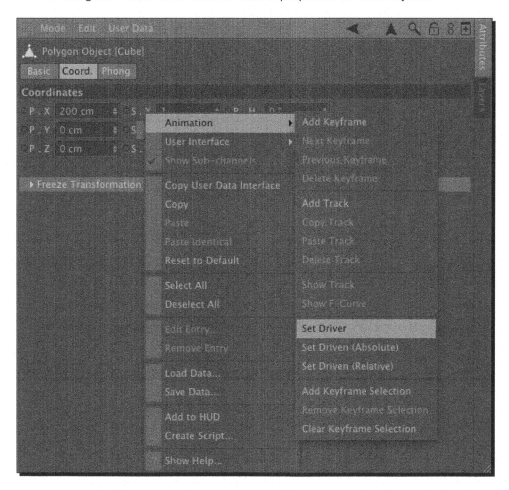

5. Select the sphere, then hold the *command* key while you select the **S. X**, **S. Y**, and **S. Z** attributes. Right-click and navigate to **Animation | Set Driven (Absolute)**.

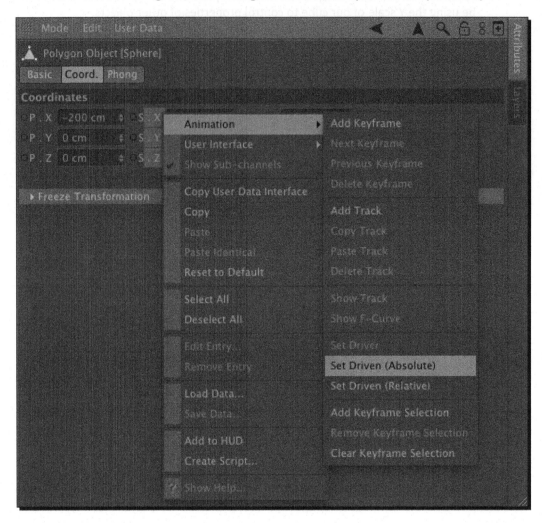

6. Select the cube and change its scale to **2**. Your sphere should automatically change to twice its original size! Note that if you select the sphere and attempt to manually change the scale, it will immediately switch back to its original value. This is because the value is being entirely driven by the Y scale of the cube, or the driver.

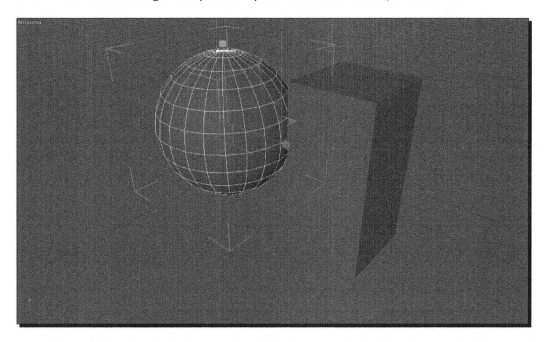

What just happened?

In your Object Manager, to the right of the sphere object, you should see a new tag:

This is an XPresso tag. By right-clicking and establishing which parameters will be the controller and which ones will be controlled, we've set up our first XPresso expression! We've linked one property (the Y scale of our cube) to another (all three scale values on our sphere). We can link that property to as many other objects as we want, as well as use more complex calculations than just a one-to-one link. If you ever forget which expressions you've defined, click on the **XPresso** tag and check the Attributes Manager. Its default name will describe which properties you've mapped to one another:

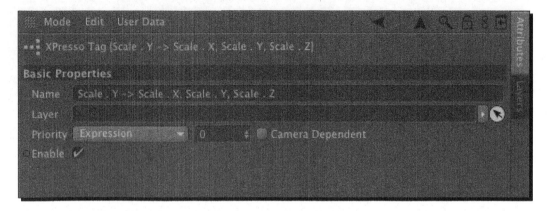

Double-click on the **XPresso** tag to open the **XPresso Editor**:

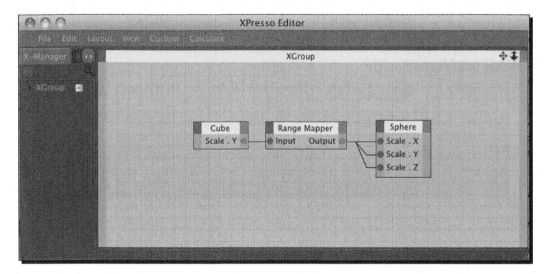

The **XPresso Editor** allows you to see and edit all of your XPresso connections, as well as create new ones. If your expressions are simple—a one-to-one relationship like the one we created earlier—you may never need to open the editor. However, it's important to understand how these relationships work, in case something needs to be re-mapped or modified.

The **Range Mapper** is created by default through the Set Driver/Set Driven method, but in this instance, it's unnecessary. Select it and delete it. (As it is connected to three separate values, you may need to select and delete multiple times.) When deleted, nothing on the screen changes—Cinema will preserve the current settings of all objects. However, if you change the Y scale of the cube, the sphere no longer changes. Click-and-drag from the pink dot on the **Cube** node to each of the three blue dots on the **Sphere** node. Now, if you scale your Y value, the sphere will update appropriately:

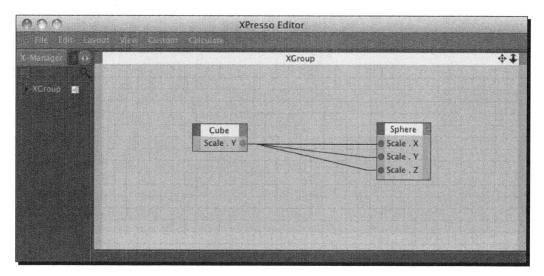

The individual boxes representing our cube and sphere are nodes, and the scale values are ports. Ports function independently and can be linked to multiple objects. Any property of an object can be added as a port by clicking on the blue or pink squares at the top of a node (blue for input, pink for output). The menu is extensive, but don't let it intimidate you! The hierarchy is well designed, so things you're looking for are easy to find. If you want to add a rotation port, for example, it's located under **Coordinates | Rotation**:

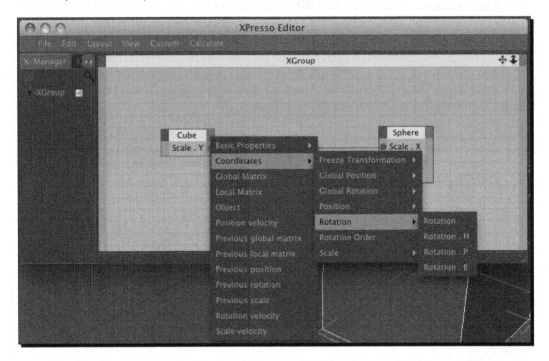

Now that we're familiar with the setup of the **XPresso Editor**, let's take things a step further and add an additional calculation.

Time for action – using Math in XPresso

Right now, our objects directly link to one another through their scale properties. If we change the Y scale of our cube to 2, the sphere's scale changes to 2 in all directions. But what if we want those values to still be linked, but not always equal to one another? Let's add a Math node that will do the work for us.

1. Right-click anywhere in the **XPresso Editor**. Navigate to **New Node | XPresso | Calculate | Math**:

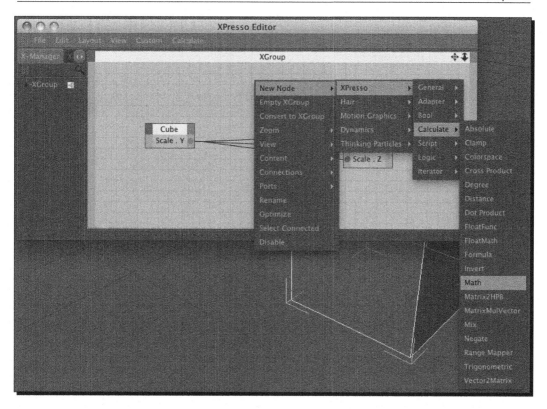

2. With the Math node selected, in the Attributes Manager change its **Function** to **Multiply**:

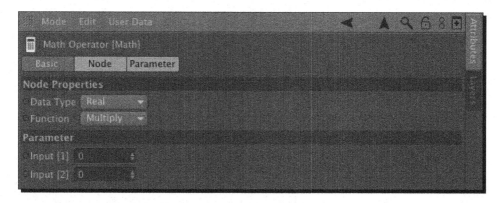

3. Draw a line from the **Scale.Y** output port on the **Cube** node to the top **Input** port on the **Math:Multiply** node. In the Attributes Manager, change the **Input [2]** value to **2**.

4. Click on each of the three lines currently connecting the cube directly to the sphere to delete them. Then, connect the **Output** port of **Math:Multiply** to all three input values of the sphere:

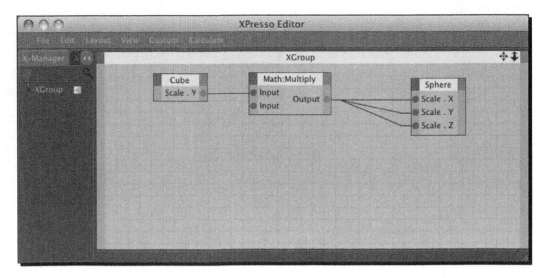

5. Now your sphere's scale will be twice the Y scale value of your cube, thanks to adding a Math node. The following screenshot shows our scene with a Y scale of 1.5 for the cube:

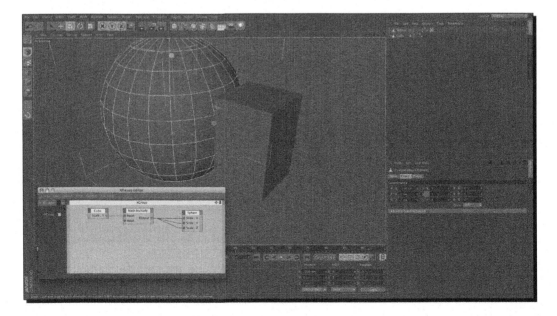

What just happened?

By adding a new node to our system, we're able to use basic mathematical calculations to maintain relative scale of objects in our scene, and allow one object's properties to control the other's. We've used scale here, but we could have easily used position and rotation as well, or all three at the same time to set up a more complex relationship.

There are thousands of uses for the Math node, and we'll continue to rely on it as we move forward through this chapter. Make sure you've saved your work so you can refer back to this basic expression if you need to reference it, because our next XPresso exercise will be mainly driven through using the Math node.

Have a go hero – create a clock

As a mini-project for this chapter, we'll use XPresso to animate the gears and hands on a clock. We'll set up a series of expressions that allow all of our individual pieces to connect to one another, by placing keyframes on one single driver.

To do this, however, we need a model of a clock! You can make this as complex or as simple as you like – it would make a nice addition to our office model. Here are some suggestions to get you started:

- We'll need gears to rotate on the back of the clock face. The easiest way to create these will be with the Cogwheel spline and an Extrude NURBS object, but you can also make unique shapes in Adobe Illustrator and import them if you prefer.

- It will be much easier to relate the cogs to one another if they are related to one another in size, that is, one cog is twice as large as another, three times larger, and so on. Try to keep your cogs as simple multiples of one another, otherwise your math will be much more complicated.

- The clock face can be created simply through a flat cylinder. If you want to include the clock in your office, you may want to add style by somehow exposing the back gears – a transparent panel may be helpful.

◆ Make sure you have an hour and a minute hand, as we'll be animating one to control the other. Adjust their axes to align with their natural rotation points by using the Axis modification tool (second last icon on your left palette), otherwise, they'll likely rotate in the center rather than from the end.

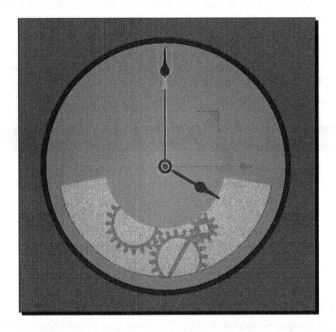

Time for action – making the gears turn

Now that you have your clock created, let's dive in and begin animating it.

1. Select the minute hand in the **Objects** Manager and add an XPresso tag (**Tags | Cinema 4D Tags | XPresso**). Double-click on the tag to open the XPresso editor. We're going to link all of our animation together with the minute hand of the clock. Let's begin by clicking and dragging the minute hand of the clock into our XPresso editor.

2. Drag the hour hand and all the cogs you created into the window as well. We'll be linking them all together, but their organization isn't important for now.

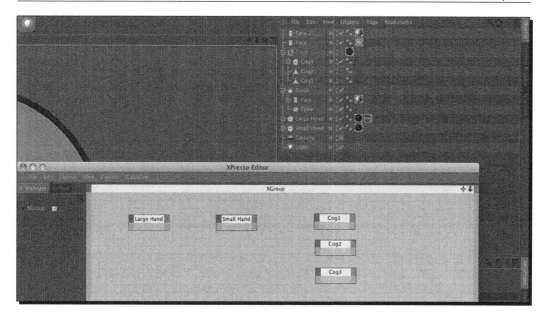

3. Let's start by linking our hour and minute hands together. Click on the pink box on your minute hand and select **Rotation . B**. (Make sure this is correct for the way you've created your objects. To double-check, try rotating your minute hand the correct way. Look in the Coordinates Manager to double-check that you've selected the correct rotation value. If your clock is aligned differently, you can either rotate the axis or simply remember for the rest of this exercise that your object is rotating on a different axis.)

4. Create a new Math node (**New Node | XPresso | Calculate | Math**). Connect the **Rotation . B** output port to the top **Input** port. In the Attributes Manager, change its **Function** to **Divide** and its **Input [2]** value to **12**:

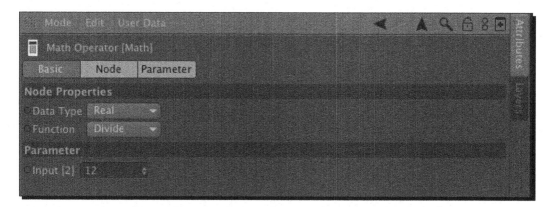

5. Add a **Rotation.B** input port to your hour hand, then link the **Output** port of the **Math:Divide** node to it:

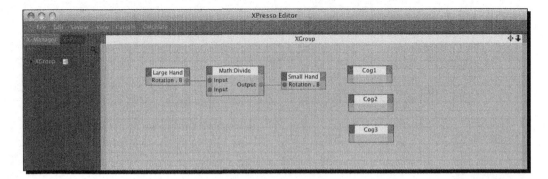

6. Now, as you rotate your minute hand, the hour hand rotates at one-twelfth the speed! We'll connect the cogs to this hand's rotation as well, but let's first relate them to one another. It was mentioned earlier that you should try and keep your cogs as simple multiples of one another, but if they aren't, you may want to attempt to make their sizes line up now. A cog that is twice the size of another will rotate exactly twice as slow (or half the speed, depending on how you'd like to think about it). The math can be calculated based on ratio, but you'll find it much easier to connect them through simpler values.

7. In the example clock, two of the cogs are exactly the same size as one another, and a third cog is half the size. Our math is going to be based on these ratios. Let's start with the largest cog (named **Cog1**) and relate it to its equal-sized cog (**Cog2**). Arrange the cogs so their teeth intersect, if they don't already:

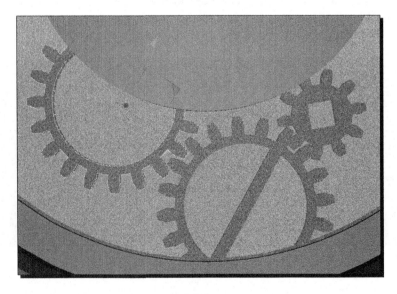

8. Add a **Rotation . B** port to your controller cog's node. (Again, make sure this is the correct rotation axis by checking the Coordinates Manager.)

9. Intersecting cogs will always rotate in opposite directions from one another—otherwise their teeth would intersect, rather than continuing to power one another. Therefore, the rotation values of identical cogs will be exact opposites of one another – if one is rotated to 90 degrees, the second should rotate to -90 degrees. Create a Math node, then connect the output of your controller cog's **Rotation . B** port to the first input value. In the Attributes Manager, change the **Function** to **Multiply**, then set **Input [2]** to **-1**:

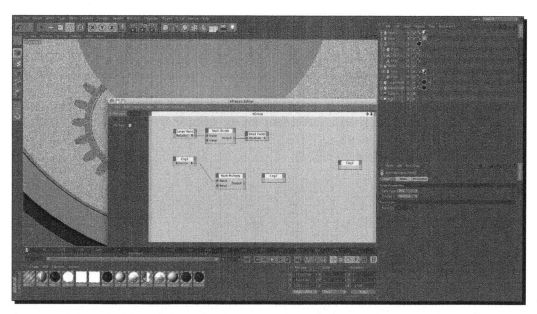

10. Add a **Rotation . B** input port to the cog you wish to control (in our example, the equal-sized cog), then connect the **Output** port of the **Math:Multiply** node to it.

11. Add a **Rotation . B** output port to the same cog. We will use this to control the third smaller cog:

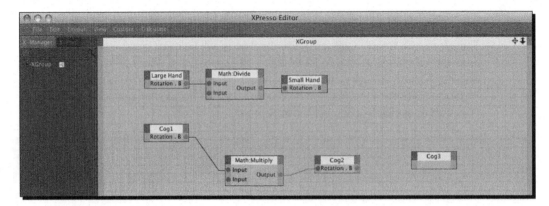

12. Add a Math node. Connect the output port of the second cog to its first **Input** port. In the Attributes Manager, set its **Function** to **Multiply**, then set its **Input [2]** value to **-2**. (Note that if your cog is three times smaller, set it to **-3**. If your cog is twice as large, it should be set to **-.5**.):

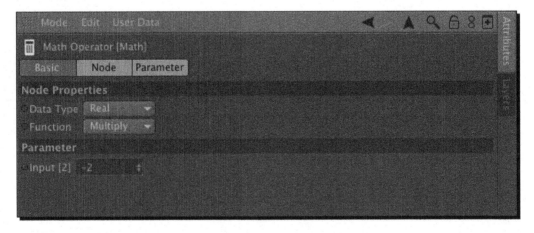

13. Add a **Rotation . B** input port to your third cog and connect it to the **Math:Multiply** output port:

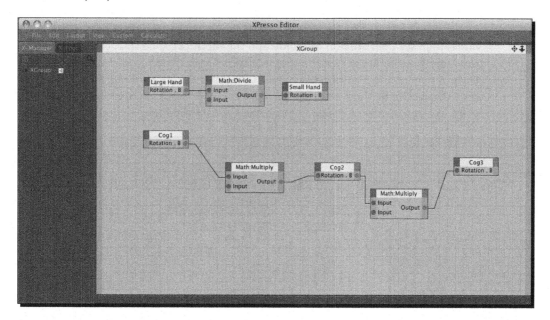

14. Now that we've connected the cogs to one another, we want them to also be linked to the minute hand, so we only have to manually animate one value to power the entire scene. Select the first cog and add a **Rotation . B** input port.

15. We could directly connect the rotation of the minute hand to the cogs by drawing a connection from the **Rotation . B** output port of the minute hand to the **Input** port for the first cog. However, to give us additional control and create additional visual interest, let's create a Math node. Connect the **Rotation . B** output port to the Math node, then set the **Function** to **Divide** and the **Input [2]** value to **2**. (This will make our largest cog rotate at half the speed of the minute hand.) Finally, connect the **Output** port on the **Math:Divide** node to the input **Rotation . B** node on the first cog. This will be the final addition we make to our XPresso expression, so if you want to clean up any of the node locations, this is a good time to do so:

16. As a final step, put everything in motion by keyframing the minute hand. The following screenshot shows a 300-frame animation from 0-720 degrees. So in 10 seconds, our clock will animate from 12:00 hours to 2:00 hours (360 degrees is one full rotation of the minute hand and it represents one hour). The higher your rotation value, the faster your clock will advance:

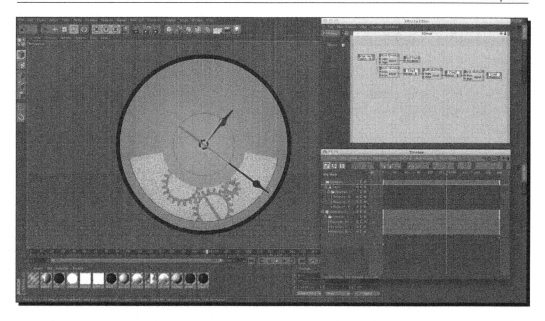

What just happened?

By using multiple Math nodes, we've created a complex backend formula that can be simply driven by animating the rotation of one single object. It may seem like an elaborate process to set up all of these constraints at first, but it will allow us so much versatility in the future that it will be worth it. We could have figured out the relative math and individually keyframed the cogs and hands. However, if we need to change something about our timing, we'll need to adjust everything individually, creating more work for ourselves and leaving more room for error. With a linked system that relies on just one variable, we can ensure consistency in our animation and make our jobs a little easier in the future.

Time for action – XPresso and MoGraph

XPresso and MoGraph are both incredibly popular tools on their own. However, all parameters of MoGraph objects can also be used in expressions. Imagine you wanted to create a Grid Cloner where the spheres inside would always be small enough to not intersect, regardless of how many clones there are inside it.

1. Create a sphere and nest it inside a Grid Cloner. Their dimensions don't matter for now, as we'll be defining some of their characteristics through XPresso.

2. Drag your **Cloner** and your **Sphere** into the **XPresso Editor**:

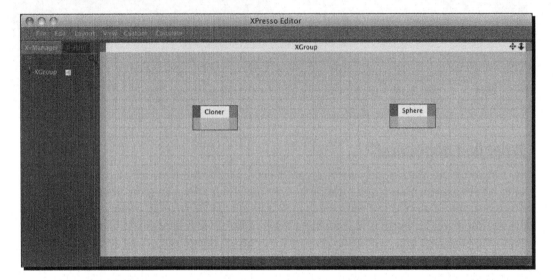

3. Create a Math node and set it to **Divide**. Add a third input port:

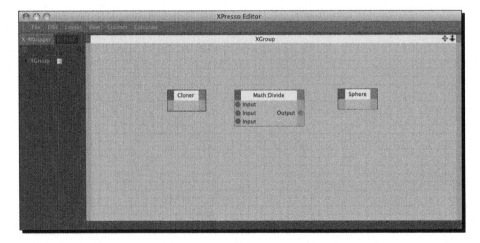

4. Add **Count** and **Size** as output ports on the **Cloner** node (**Object Properties | Count** and **Object Properties | Size**). Add a **Radius** input port to the **Sphere** node (**Object Properties | Radius**).

5. Connect **Size** to **Input [1]** and **Count** to **Input [2]**. In the Attributes Manager, change **Input [3]** to **2**. Then, connect the **Output** port of **Math:Divide** to the **Radius** input port. This takes the size of the Cloner and divides it by the number of clones, then divides that number by **2**. The result is the new radius of our sphere. As you increase the size and count on the **Cloner**, your spheres will always be this ratio apart from one another, as determined by the **Input [3]** value:

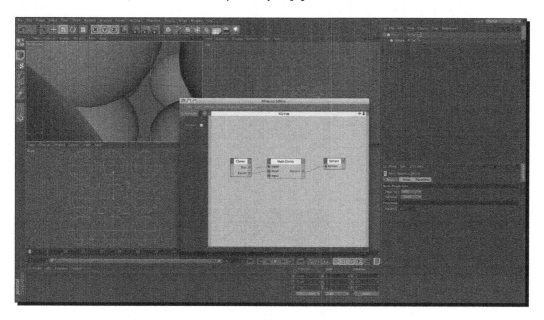

6. Now that we've linked our basic parameters, let's set up some interface commands that keep us from having to adjust our XPresso settings. Since we've set up a basic system already, our next task is to visually represent it in a better, friendlier way. Create a Null object and parent the **Cloner** to it. Then, in the **XPresso Editor**, select the **Math:Divide** node. Right-click on **Input [3]** and select **Copy User Data Interface**. This lets C4D know that we want to represent this node of our system in the next step:

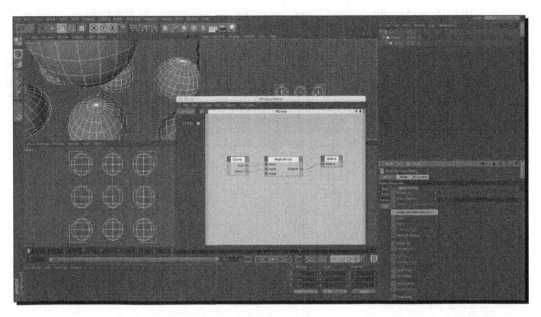

7. Select the Null object, and in the Attributes Manager, navigate to **User Data | Paste User Data Interface....** Click on **OK** to dismiss the pop-up window for now:

8. You should now see a new tab called **User Data** on your Null object. Right-click on **Input [3]** and navigate to **Animation | Set Driver**. Then, select the **Math:Divide** node in your **XPresso Editor**, and in the Attributes Manager, right-click on **Input [3]** and navigate to **Animation | Set Driven (Absolute). Now**. If you change the **Input [3]** value in your User Data, your Cloner's settings will change, without even having to touch the **XPresso Editor**!

9. Let's make one more change to make things easier. Right-click on **Input [3]** and then navigate to **User Interface | Float Slider**:

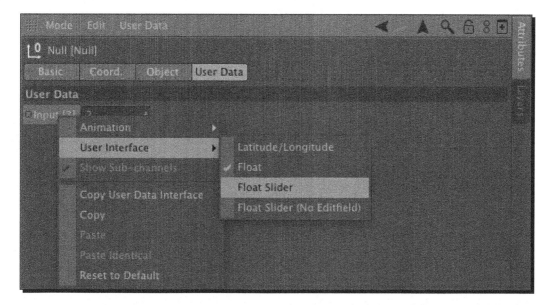

10. If you move the slider we just created, you'll notice that the values increase very, very quickly. It's very unlikely that we'll ever want to use such massive values, so let's set up a couple of defining parameters. Right-click on **Input [3]** again and select **Edit Entry**. Change the **Limit Min** value to **1** (remember that we're dividing, and we don't want to divide by zero!) and change the **Limit Max** value to **10**. Click on the **Slider Min** and **Slider Max** checkboxes, and they will automatically update with the larger values. If you ever want to divide by more than 10, you can open this menu again – or, if you anticipate dividing by more than that, you can change your maximum value now, and you'll be able to enter that value manually even if the slider does not go as high. Set the **Default Value** field to **2** and click on **OK**.

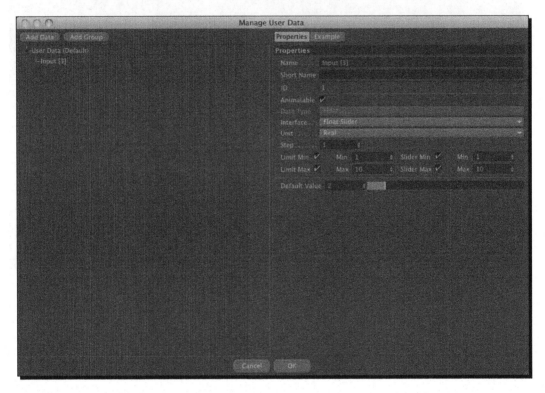

Now, you have a much more reasonable slider to work with!

What just happened?

We discussed how powerful it is to combine tools in *Chapter 7, MoGraph*, and now we're able to see that again as we combine MoGraph with XPresso. We've also learned how to use User Data to take things one step further. We began by using MoGraph to create complex animations, then learned how XPresso can help us link properties together and simplify our keyframing, and now we've combined everything together into a simple slider to make everything work together with the click of a button.

Summary

We've covered a lot of ground in this chapter, but we've only scratched the surface of what XPresso can do! The C4D online community is very helpful, so if you come up with a task that you think might be easy to accomplish through XPresso, consider doing some basic research before you begin building it. Online resources such as C4D Cafe are well known for offering helpful advice and examples of time-saving scripts. Just remember to take things one step at a time and work through them logically, and you'll be setting up complex behaviors through simple, customizable expressions in no time.

In this chapter, we covered how to set properties of objects as controllers for other objects, how to access and edit expressions through the XPresso editor, ways to link properties and parameters through XPresso. Also, how to take properties of an object and apply mathematical calculations to return different variables and define other objects and how to create sliders to more easily control variables without having to navigate the XPresso editor.

The next chapter will introduce some additional modules very briefly, to give you a general overview of some additional tools you may have at your disposal. All of these modules will be included in the Studio installation of Cinema 4D, but many of them are located in the Broadcast and Visualize packages as well.

9

An Overview of Additional Tools

Cinema 4D offers four basic packages: Prime, Broadcast, Visualize, and Studio. Which tool you choose depends on the jobs you need to accomplish! We'll take a look at various additional modules that enhance Cinema's toolset to help you decide which package best suits your workflow.

In this chapter we will learn about:

- Hair
- Sketch and Toon
- Cloth

Time for action – hair

Unique to the Studio installation, Cinema 4D's Hair tools allow you to add realistic hair and fur to your objects. This is particularly useful for anyone interested in character animation, but has less common applications such as realistic grass and trailing particle effects.

1. Let's begin by creating a sphere.

2. Select the sphere and navigate to **Simulate | Hair Objects | Add Hair**.

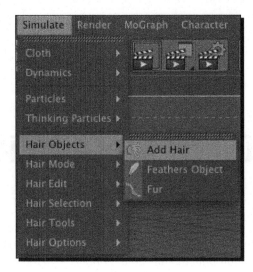

Just like that, you've added hair to an object!

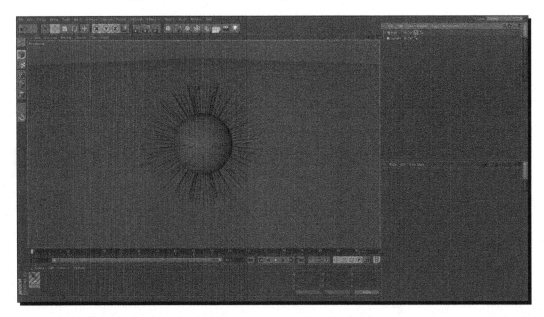

3. Render your current view to take a look at the actual appearance of the object:

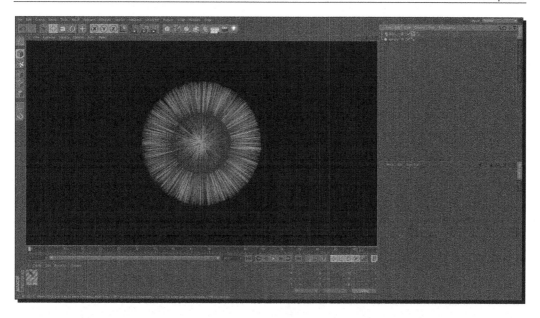

What we have so far doesn't look too realistic. However, the Hair object has one very important feature that we should examine. Much like the MoGraph module, Hair objects are fully integrated with dynamics! Hit play, or scroll your playhead through the timeline to see how the Hair object changes over time:

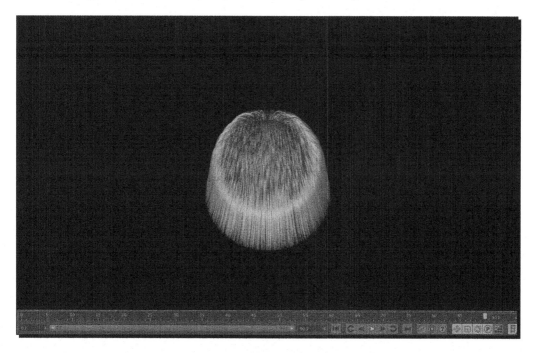

The behavior of the falling hair can be controlled via the **Dynamics** tab in the Attributes Manager:

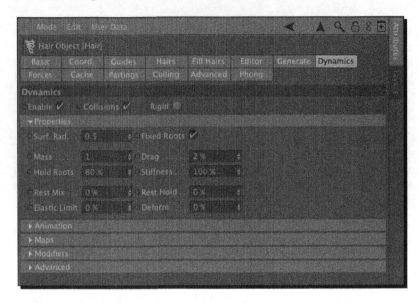

4. Changing the **Stiffness** value from **100%** to **0%** results in a much finer hair appearance – hair is still attached at the same roots, but has far less body and will hang straighter:

5. Rendering Hair objects is very processor-intensive. To combat this problem while working on a file, Cinema differentiates between **Guides** and **Hairs**:

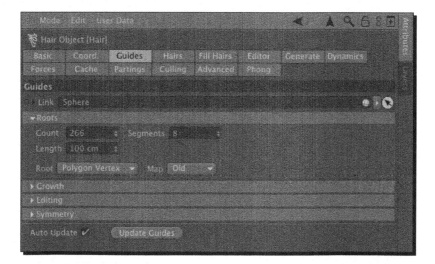

By default, objects have 266 guides and 5000 hairs. Each of the 266 guides represents an individual hair, and the additional hairs are filled in by interpolating behavior from one guide to the next. This results in an overall smoothness that is far less taxing on your processor. If you need further control over hairs, you can increase the **Count** value in the Attributes Manager under**Guides** | **Roots**.

6. If we were working with an actual character rather than just a sample sphere, we would most likely find our current Hairs count to be too low – we're seeing the sphere through the hair. To create denser hair, select the **Hairs** tab and increase the count until you achieve the desired look:

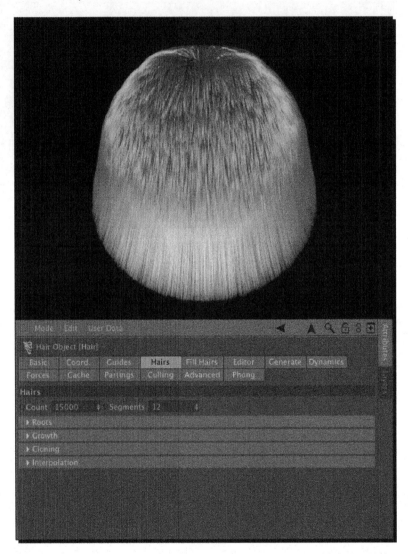

7. Optionally, if you need a fuller hair look, you can add **Fill Hairs**. This is a less processor-intensive task, but creates a slightly different look. Compare the following screenshot which uses **Fill Hairs** to the previous screenshot created entirely with a higher Hairs count. Hairs are better at realistically interpreting behavior, but if you need fullness on a time budget, **Fill Hairs** can be a very helpful option:

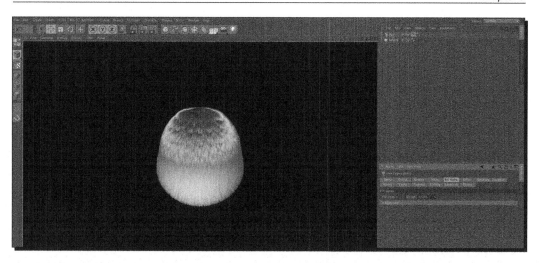

What just happened?

We're becoming familiar with the basic attributes of a Hair object, but we've just scratched the surface on understanding how to create the look we're going for.

In the previous screenshots and the scene you've created, you'll notice that our Hair object not only has multiple hairs, but also appears shiny, has thickness, and has a natural color variation found in human hair. In addition to the dynamics settings on the Hair object itself, much of the behavior of individual hairs is controlled by the Hair material:

When you add a Hair object to a scene, a Hair material is automatically created. This allows you to change the color of your hairs, control how shiny they are via **Specular**, and control their **Thickness** (as well as allow for variation in all three to add realism). As you can see in the previous screenshot, you can also add curl, wave, frizz, and many other properties to create the exact custom look you desire. Take a look at the following screenshot with additional parameters turned on to see how very different your hair can look due to changing material settings alone!

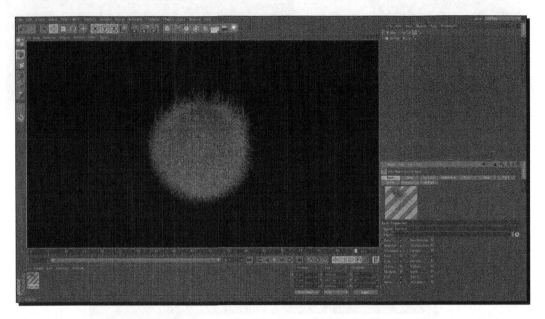

Time for action – hair materials without Hair objects

Hair materials can also be applied directly to an object without creating a separate Hair object. This is particularly effective for creating something like grass or fur, where the number of hairs and dynamic control is less necessary. Note that if you create an object in this fashion, you will not see any **Guides** and will only see your hair material at render time.

1. Duplicate your hair material and delete the sphere. Instead, create a plane and assign the hair material to it:

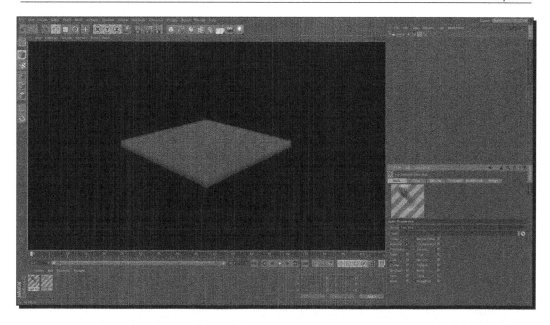

2. Enable the **Frizz** and **Bend** options (their default settings are fine for now). Change both swatches in the **Color** gradient to offset shades of green. This can be done with custom colors you choose, or you can very simply change them by double-clicking on the color swatch, changing the 30 degree value to 100, clicking on **OK**, and making the same modification to the second swatch. The offset will be the same as the default brown value, just in a different hue:

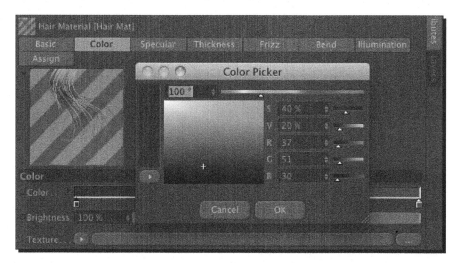

3. The current specular value is set too high, so let's select the **Specular** tab and change the value of the **Strength** field of the **Primary** and **Secondary** specular values, as well as **Back Specular**, to **10 %**:

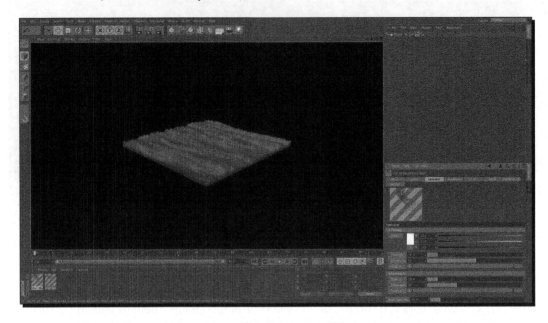

4. One problem we face is that we can still see our plane through the grass. Depending on the level of detail necessary, we can create a dirt-like texture and also add it to the plane. Alternatively, add a display tag to the plane (in the **Objects** Manager, navigate to **Tags | Cinema 4D | Display**), then in the Attributes Manager, enable **Visibility** and change the value to **0%**:

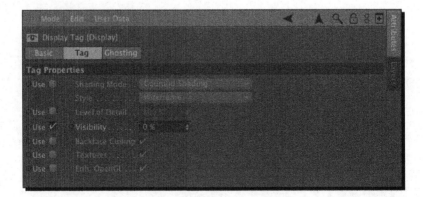

Now when we render, we don't see the plane underneath, and only see the grass!

What just happened?

We've learned how to liberate materials from objects, allowing ourselves a way to create realistic-looking hair in situations where animation and detail may not be as necessary. This allows us to just focus on the quality of the material without worrying about assigning number of hairs and their behavior, since Hair materials are so powerful on their own.

Sketch and Toon

So far, as we've created materials and lighting, we've done our best to render objects realistically. However, Cinema is capable of producing non-photorealistic rendering as well – that's where Sketch and Toon comes in! Sketch and Toon encompasses a large toolset that can be used for achieving everything from cartoonish animation to technical diagrams. It is part of the Visualize and Studio installations.

Time for action – placing accurate lighting

Now, we'll add a non-photorealistic style to our scene using Sketch and Toon. A rendered still of the sample scene is as follows:

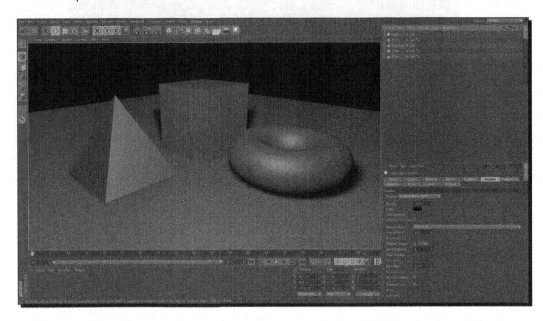

1. Open your **Render Settings**, then navigate to **Effect | Sketch and Toon**.

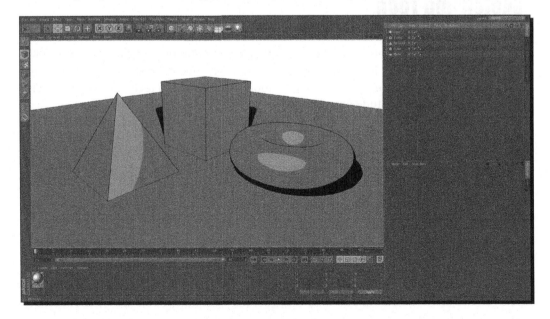

2. Now, when you render, everything in your scene looks like it's been cell rendered – like a cartoon! You'll also notice, similar to the Hair object, that there is now a Sketch Material in your Materials Manager.

> Sketch and Toon, by default, will render a cartoonish version of everything in your scene. The material that was just automatically created is the new default texture for the scene – much like the medium gray, low-specular texture that shows up on your objects if they are untextured, but now you have the option to select that default material and change its settings.

3. Create a new material and change its color to red (255,0,0). Do not change any additional settings. Assign the new material to one of your objects.

4. Duplicate the sketch material. Then, select the **Color** tab in the Attributes Manager and change its color to blue (0,0,255).

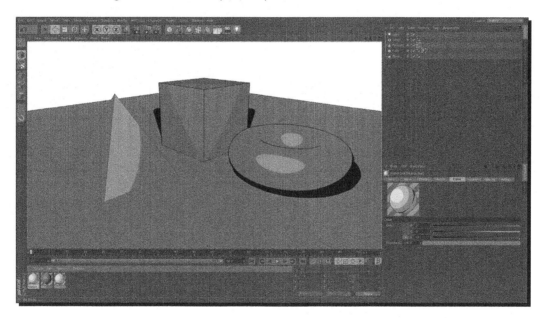

What just happened?

We now have a style for our scene that is working with objects in three separate ways.

The torus on the right has no material assigned, so all of its attributes are being taken from the default, original material created when we added the Sketch and Toon effect. The cube in the center has a standard material assigned to it to control the color of its faces. However, its outlines are black because it is getting its stroke information from the same default material as the torus. The pyramid on the left has a second sketch material assigned to it, giving it a bright blue outline.

Note that in the Objects Manager, there is a new tag assigned to the pyramid that looks different from a **Texture tag**. This **Sketch Style** tag operates independently, so we can assign both standard and sketch materials to an individual object. In the following screenshot, the blue outline is now assigned to the red cube. Its face color is unaffected, but it is no longer relying on the default black outline.

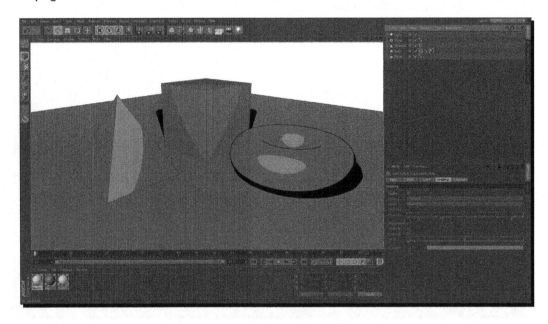

Time for action – global settings and materials

In Sketch and Toon, there is a balance to strike between which settings to change in standard materials, which to change in sketch materials, and which to change globally. Almost any setting can be changed at either a global level or a material level. Which one you change on a case-by-case basis depends on the style you're attempting to create. If you're working on a technical diagram and attempting to create a hand-drawn colored pencil style, you will most likely want to create a number of different sketch materials. If you're creating a cartoon, you may want everything to maintain a consistent black outline and color your objects through a series of standard materials.

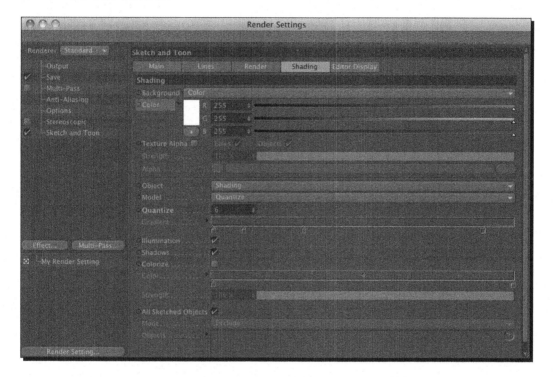

1. Global Sketch and Toon settings are controlled through the **Render Settings** window. The **Quantize** option allows you to customize how shading is interpreted. Right now, with a value of **6**, each of our objects appears very flat and has a simple, hard-defined highlight. If we change the value to something higher – say, **20** – each object begins to have much more complicated, stair-stepped highlights:

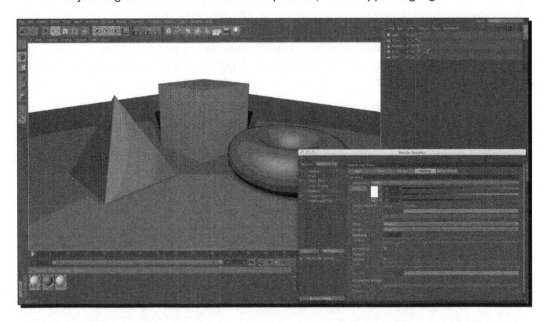

2. The **Render** tab allows you to specify anti-aliasing for your outlines. This should generally be set to **Best**, unless you find your render times become too high:

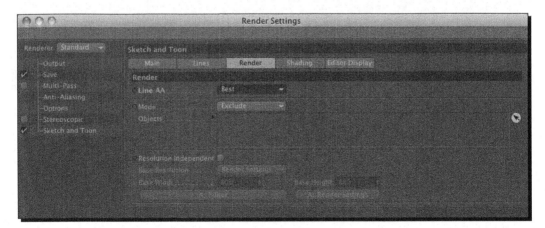

3. The **Editor Display** tab allows you to see your lines in the viewport by enabling **Show Lines**. All lines will be a uniform color and thickness by default, but you can enable **Line Color** as well as **Line Thickness**, to allow the sketch materials to override it:

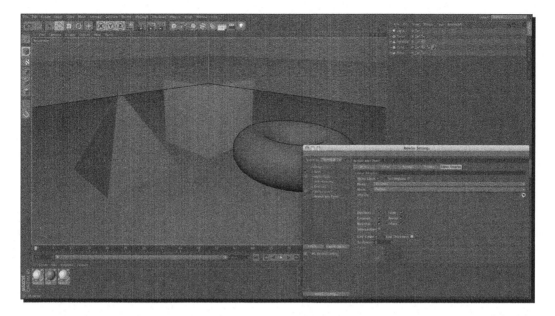

4. Let's delete the sketch tags from our pyramid and cube, as well as the blue outline material, and allow all of our objects to be globally controlled.

5. In the **Main** tab of the sketch material, you can scroll through a number of preset materials that will dramatically change the appearance of your scene. If you have enabled **Show Lines**, you will be able to see a basic preview, but your render may end up looking quite different. You can choose from themes such as:

    ❑   Brush

    ❑   Charcoal

    ❑   Marker

    ❑   Pen

    ❑   Technical

    There are many more themes, as well as variations on all of the previous ones.

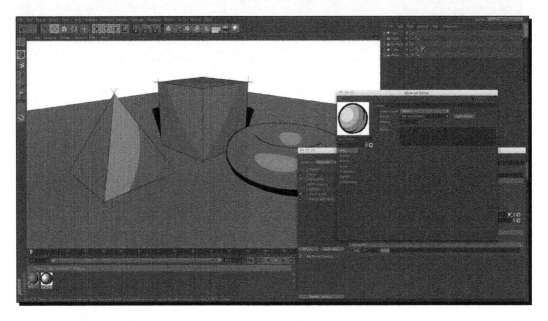

6. It's worth experimenting with multiple options to find what works best for your scene. For example, in the previous screenshot, the overshoot style works well for the cube and pyramid, but looks awkward as it rounds the corners of the torus. In this case, we could choose another style, or create a separate material for rounded objects. It's best to make these decisions early on in the modeling stage so you can consider your end product as you work.

7. Instead of using the **Pen (Overshoot)** style, take a look at **Felt (Thin)**. It will give you some of the overlap that looks good in the previous style, but will work a little better on the curves. Its default color is bright red; change it to black in the **Color** tab.

8. Under the **Main** tab, above the **Preset** field, change the **Control Level** value to **Advanced**. This opens up a number of additional options, including a new **Animate** tab! Select the **Animate** tab and enable the **Draw** option. Now, let's take a look at our animation options:

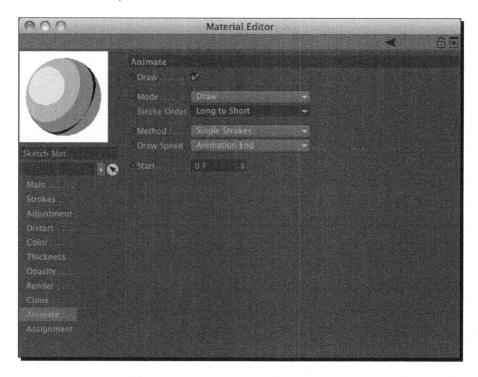

9. Enabling the **Draw** option will build your scene from scratch over any period of time you specify, stroke by stroke, in any order you choose. This is one of the most powerful options in Sketch and Toon – what would take hours to manually animate in other pieces of software is done here for you with the click of a button and a couple of setting choices!

What just happened?

We've examined the difference between options that can be controlled globally for a Sketch and Toon scene, and we've looked at how we can add style with pre-defined materials. We've also learned about the option for animation.

In *Chapter 10, Optimizing Your Workflow*, we'll discuss further compositing options in Adobe After Effects. The **Animate** option will make all kinds of creative options possible, such as an animated mechanical drawing with the **Tech** preset, or transitioning from a drawn-on cartoonish preset to a photorealistic animation.

If you've ever used 2D image creation software that works with layering modes (Multiply, Overlay, Screen, and so on), you would know how much can be done with a simple black and white outline. This can be quickly created in Cinema through Sketch and Toon. Set the color on your material to black, then re-open the **Render Settings** window. Under the **Shading** tab, change the **Object** shading mode to **Custom Color**, then change the color to white (if it isn't already set as white by default).

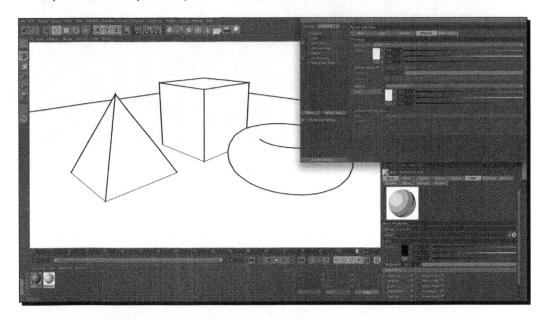

With one render setting and a couple of basic choices in the Attributes Manager, we've created a completely different, fully-animated look and feel for our scene!

Cloth

Take a look at a piece of cloth – a tablecloth, or a piece of clothing draped over another object. Fabric, like many organic objects, can be very difficult to replicate by hand in 3D space. This is where Cinema 4D's cloth engine comes in – it simulates realistic fabric behavior with a couple of simple steps.

Time for action – creating a cloth object

1. Let's create a new scene with a cube and a plane. Move the plane to **110** cm on the Y axis so it sits just above the cube, and then make it editable.

2. With the plane selected, navigate to **Tags | Simulation Tags | Cloth**. Then, select the cube and add a **Cloth Collider** tag using the same menu:

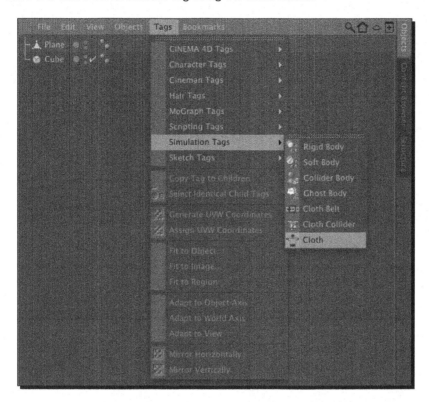

3. Select the Cloth tag on the plane and click on **Relax**. Render your viewport and take a look!

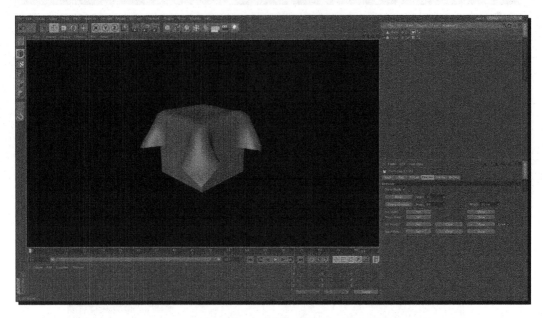

4. As you can see, we've started to create a realistic-looking tablecloth. However, we've got a couple of problems that can be remedied in a number of ways. The first major issue is that our corners aren't quite draping the way we'd like them to. One solution is to nest the plane within a HyperNURBS object. You'll notice that the corners of the cube stick through when we do this, but that's a fixable problem.

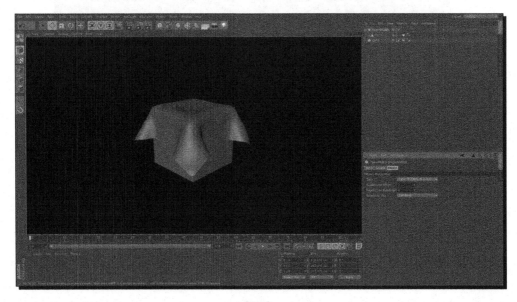

5. The HyperNURBS solution isn't a bad one, but we have other options as well. Un-parent the plane from the HyperNURBS object, then delete the HyperNURBS. Since we haven't made any modifications other than relaxing the plane, let's reset it by unchecking the **Dress Mode** checkbox. Once it's reset, you can click on the **Set** button next to **Init State**, allowing us to see the plane in its original form at any time without having to re-relax it.

6. Let's experiment with the relax options. Change the steps to a higher number; the following screenshot will show **50**. If your computer ran slowly when you relaxed it with 10 steps, you may want to use a lower number (the 20-30 range should be sufficient). You'll notice that our fabric slides around and becomes less rigid, but we still have a problem with jagged edges:

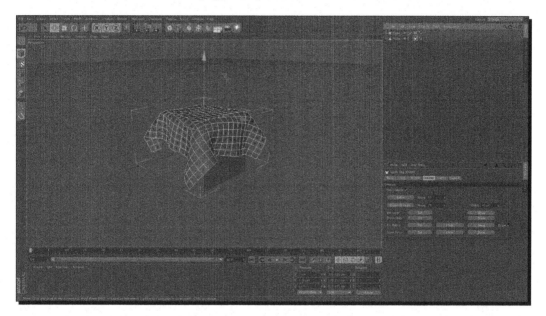

7. Return the plane to its initial state. Switch to Polygon Mode, then select all polygons (*command + A* on your keyboard). Navigate to **Mesh | Commands** and then click on the box to the right of **Subdivide** to open the options menu:

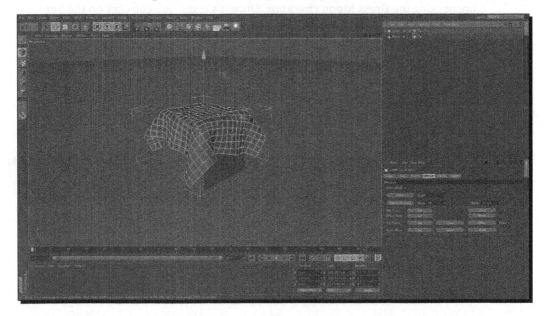

8. On the new **Subdivide** menu, set the **Subdivision** value to **2**. One of the biggest problems we've had so far with our cloth object is that we haven't given it enough information to work – polygons can't bend in the middle! Now we have many more options:

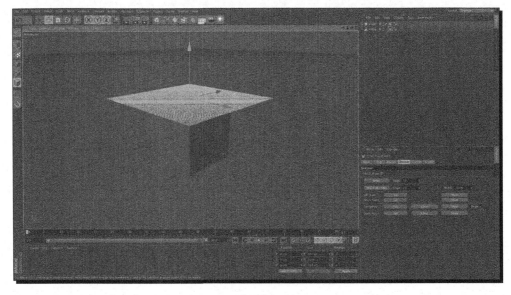

9. Select the Cloth Tag, lower the number of steps (15 is sufficient), and click on **Relax**:

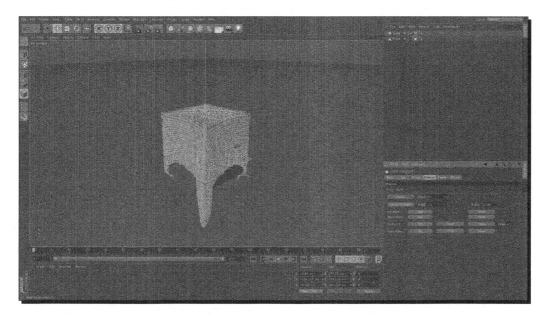

10. Now we've got more options to work with, but giving the plane that many subdivisions has lost some of the body we originally had. Let's reduce the steps to 10 (make sure to uncheck the **Dress Mode** box first, otherwise you'll add 10 steps on to where we are right now).

11. The corners of our object are still a problem. One additional solution, if the intersection of the cloth and the underlying geometry is causing issues, is to change the geometry it's set to collide with. Select the cube and enable the **Fillet** option. Change the radius to 20 cm. Reset the plane, then relax it:

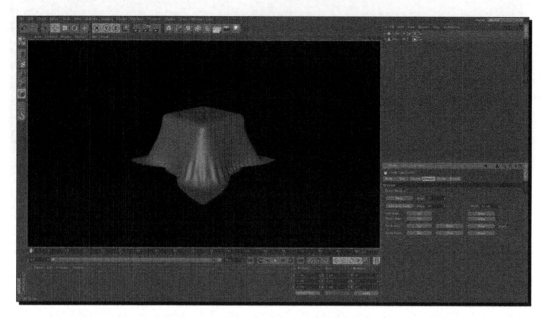

12. Our object is looking better, but we may still want to parent it to a HyperNURBS object with a low subdivision to smooth out some of our edges.

The **Tag** tab also offers a number of options to help control how the cloth behaves as it falls.

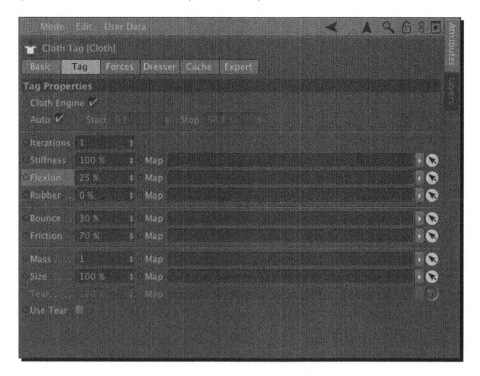

 You may want to create a new plane and work with less polygons as you experiment with variables, as well as turn off the HyperNURBS object while the Relax state is occurring. This will be less processor-intensive.

What just happened?

By adding tags to our objects, we've taught them to behave in a certain way. This is one of Cinema 4D's main strengths – the built-in dynamics functions allow for complex behavior by defining a series of basic physical properties, and then the physics are simulated for you! Using cloth objects is a quick way to add realism to interior scenes.

Summary

This chapter has introduced us to some complex objects in a very short amount of time. Remember that all the things we've learned here can be combined with what we've learned so far – anything can be keyed, Sketch and Toon can be used to add non-photorealistic style to any of your MoGraph scenes, and hair can be added to any object! One of Cinema's strengths is how easily all of its individual tools integrate with one another.

In this chapter, we covered:

◆   How to add hair and fur to objects

◆   How to use Sketch and Toon to achieve different styles

◆   How to quickly create realistic-looking cloth objects

Our next and final chapter will wrap up everything we've learned so far and discuss potential next steps for your scenes. In professional animation, renders are rarely used directly out of Cinema – we've taken the first step and made things as realistic as we can, but we'll take what we've made so far and integrate it with external programs such as Adobe After Effects and Adobe Photoshop to add just a little more pop to our scenes.

If you don't have these programs, there's still something in the next chapter for you! We'll discuss scene optimization a little further, as well as learn about Xrefs and discuss compositing and display tags. These tags are most commonly used for exporting to third-party software, but have numerous benefits if Cinema is your final step as well.

Congratulations on how far you've come! The next chapter is just icing on the cake.

10
Optimizing Your Workflow

In our final chapter, we'll discuss how to best optimize your project files and renders to save your time and make your process easier. We'll also discuss the next steps with your renders—how to take what you've created and turn it into a beautiful final product.

In this chapter we will learn about:

- ◆ XRefs
- ◆ Compositing tags
- ◆ Multipass rendering
- ◆ Exporting to Adobe After Effects and Adobe Photoshop

Before we begin

Instead of creating something new, we'll work through the concepts in this chapter using some of the files we've already created. Make sure that you have your office scene handy!

We'll be using Adobe After Effects to work with our animated files, and we'll use Adobe Photoshop to work on a still image. If you don't have either of these software applications, 30-day trial versions can be downloaded from Adobe's website. If you use a different image editor (such as GIMP, a freeware program), it is possible that some of the concepts will apply.

This chapter will walk you through the steps of enhancing your renders in these two software applications, but will not cover the basics. A beginner level of proficiency is assumed.

XRefs

If you've ever worked with CAD software, you may be familiar with XRefs. XRefs allow you to embed `.c4d` files within one another. If you were working on a series of scenes that will all use the same desk, you could select the model and copy and paste it into each individual file. Imagine, though, that you want to make a change to that desk and have it apply across the board—you'd have to modify the desk, then open each file, paste the model, and reposition it accordingly.

XRefs allow you to simplify this process. By creating a file that contains the desk and using XRefs, you can update countless files at once. It's as if Cinema has created an instance of the desk instead of an editable copy.

Remember that we animated the lighting in this scene, so when you open your file, you may see total darkness. You can scrub through the timeline in order to turn the lights on if you're having trouble, or delete the first animation keyframes entirely for the purposes of this exercise. Make sure you save your file as a copy if you delete the animation!

Time for action – creating XRefs

XRefs can be created in two different ways. Let's open our office model and start exploring:

1. Open your office scene. Select one of the two chairs in front of the desk, (if you created multiple chairs, make sure the one you've selected isn't an instance).

2. Navigate to **Create | XRef | Convert Object Selection to XRef**:

3. You will be prompted to save your file. Creating an XRef will make a separate `.c4d` file. You can name it anything you wish, but it's best to keep `xref_` at the beginning of the name so it will be differentiated in your folder. When you create multiple XRefs, it'll be easy to spot which files are which in your folder. Also, if you're using external images in your materials, you'll want to make sure you keep your project files close together so they can all reference the same texture folder.

4. Once you've created your XRef, you'll be prompted to open the new project. Select **Yes** as shown in the next screenshot, and let's look at what we've created:

5. Your new file should contain just the chair, as well as any materials that were assigned to it. You'll notice that the chair is in its position from the original file. Let's change its X and Z position to 0 (leaving the Y position where it is to ensure that it still sits on the floor) and reset all rotation keyframes to 0 as well. This will require us to move it in the original file, but if we want to use this XRef in another file, our axis point will be at the center of the chair instead of a few meters away. Save the XRef file:

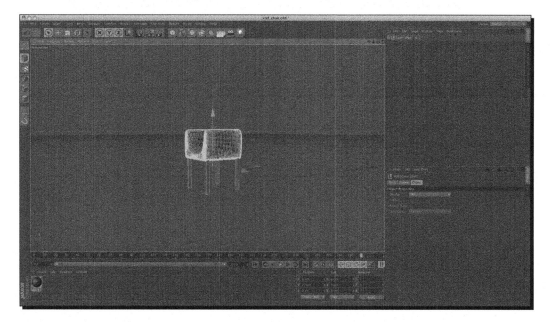

6. Return to the original office scene. Your chair will most likely still be in the same position for now, if you save your file and re-open it though, it will have moved, so let's go ahead and update it correctly now. Select the XRef in the Objects Manager, then click on **Reload** in the Attributes Manager:

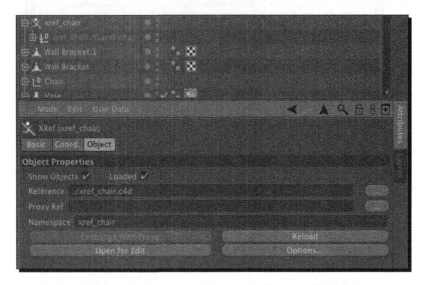

7. The chair has most likely shifted position to be right in the center of the desk, so update its position and rotation accordingly.

8. To keep our project file tidy, let's have both desk chairs use the same XRef. Delete the extra chair. We can (and should, in most cases) just copy and paste the XRef, but let's use this opportunity to learn how to add a new XRef instead. Navigate to **Create | XRef | Add XRef....** In the pop-up dialog, navigate to and select the XRef project file:

9. The new XRef is again in the center of our desk, so reposition and rotate it to fit with the rest of the scene.

What just happened?

In a couple of easy steps, we've organized our file and given ourselves a way to link things together! Now, we can use this desk chair in as many scenes as we wish. XRefs are simple to create, but offer a number of advanced options. A few things to keep in mind:

♦ If you make a modification to any object within XRef, they will apply to all files that reference it. Most 3D animators will, over time, develop a reference library—once you've made a chair, you don't want your hard work to go to waste, and you don't want to waste your time by creating new models when an old one would do just fine (or at least be a good starting point). It's possible to just constantly reference objects in your personal library, however, remember that if you make a specific modification for the scene you're working on, it will then apply to every other file that references it. When you begin a new project, you may want to make a copy of the file so that you don't disturb older projects you've worked on.

♦ XRefs have a unique appearance in the Objects Manager, but you can also see a list of just reference objects in the **XRef Manager**. This manager has a unique location; instead of finding it under the **Window** tab, navigate to **Create | XRef | XRef Manager**. Here, you can easily peruse all of your XRefs rather than hunting them down in the Objects Manager:

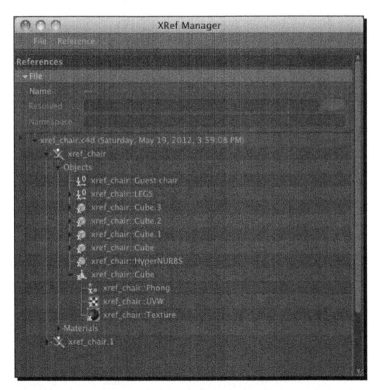

◆ Certain parameters of XRefs can be changed, such as the position, scale, and rotation of individual objects within the XRef. If you select one of the chair legs, you'll notice that you can move it around. If you want to protect your XRefs and make sure that these modifications aren't possible, select the XRef and open the **Options** dialog in the Attributes Manager. Under the **Modify** tab, uncheck the box for **PSR** (position, scale, rotation) and click on **OK**, as shown in the following screenshot:

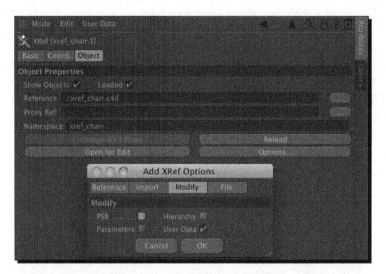

◆ When you have an XRef in a scene, its materials will appear in the Materials Manager. If you select one of these materials, however, you will be unable to edit it in the Attributes Manager. All of its parameters will be deselected and cannot be activated.

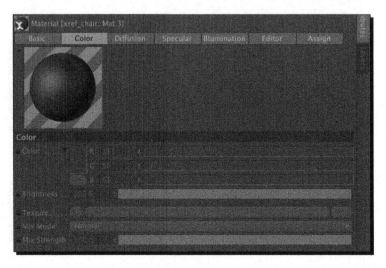

Understanding the importance of compositing

We've discussed Cinema's external compositing capabilities, but you may be wondering what are the benefits of bringing in a second piece of software to finish the job. These benefits are as follows:

◆ Rendering out of Cinema 4D is time-consuming. Imagine you're working on a scene that has a television screen on the wall. The screen will be playing an animation that you've created elsewhere, or a video given to you by a client. Cinema can handle animated textures, so you could take a Quicktime movie and add it into the color (and most likely luminance) channel on a new material. After rendering, however, you realize the video you've chosen to put on the screen really isn't working as well as you'd like. To change it, you'll have to redo the entire render and if you've got a complex scene, that could take hours or even days.

◆ A better strategy would be to create your television within the scene and add the video as a separate layer within Adobe After Effects. This means that the only re-rendering you'll need to do will be out of After Effects instead of re-doing the Cinema render, which will save you a significant amount of time. This allows you the freedom to change elements along the way without constantly worrying about time constraints.

◆ You can also separate out elements of your scene into separate layers, allowing for high-level visual control in post production without modifying your 3D scene. Worried that your lights may need to be brighter or are too bright? Shadows might be too dark, or not dark enough? By rendering these layers out as separate passes, you can change their intensity and add post effects after your render is complete, without going back in and enduring long render times as you modify the original scene.

◆ Cinema 4D makes these tasks simple with just a couple of extra steps. Let's open up our office scene and add in a couple of elements to get it ready for post production!

Time for action – modeling for compositing

To get started, let's add an object to our scene that will work well for post-processing. Let's add a television screen and hang it on the wall of our office.

1. Create a cube that is **132 cm** x **75 cm** x **4 cm**. Place it on one of the walls in the office:

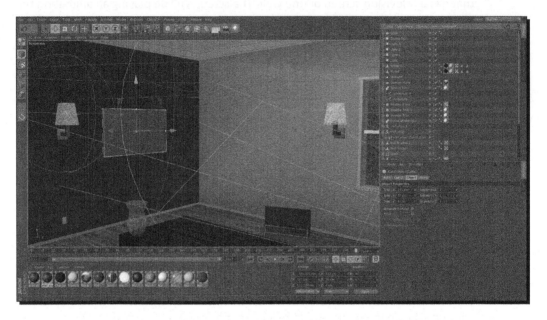

2. Make the cube editable, then select the front face. Use the **Extrude Inner** command with an **Offset** of **3 cm** to create a frame around the screen:

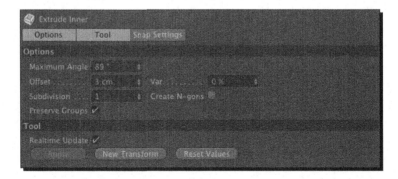

3. Using the **Extrude** command, offset the currently selected panel (which should be the center face, representing the screen) by **-3 cm**:

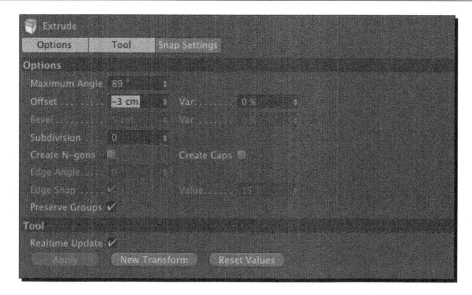

4. Right-click on the screen face and select the **Split** command from the list. This will create a separate object for just the screen. Rename the new object **Screen**, then set it as a child of the television object:

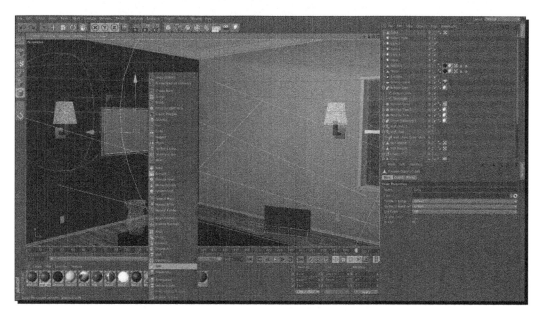

5. Create two new materials: A black material with mid-range specular for the television frame, and a white material with 50 percent luminance for the screen. Assign them to the appropriate objects. You may want to move the new screen panel slightly forward from its original position so that the white material shows through:

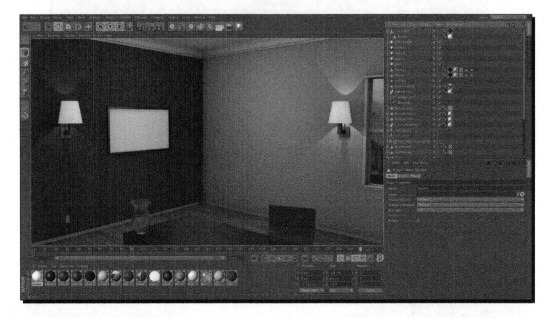

What just happened?

We've created an object in our scene that can be used for compositing in post-production. Since screen images won't benefit much from things like Global Illumination or materials (as they're defining their own material), and they're often prone to last-minute content changes, it often makes more sense to composite onscreen images in a 3D scene in postproduction rather than rendering them directly out of Cinema.

Any content such as infographics, typography, or other 2D animations that appear in 3D scenes will often be much easier in post-production. And often, if you've created the 2D animation, you can simply use the preexisting composition and skip the After Effects rendering stage.

Time for action – compositing tags

Now that we've got an object that will work well for compositing, we'll need to add a couple of tags to let After Effects know how to interpret the scene.

1. Select the screen object (not the television!). In the Objects Manager, navigate to **Tags** | **CINEMA 4D Tags** | **Compositing**, as shown in the following screenshot:

2. In the Attributes Manager, select the **Object Buffer** tab, then click on the top checkbox to enable **Buffer 1**. You can choose any number you like, but make sure you remember it for the next step:

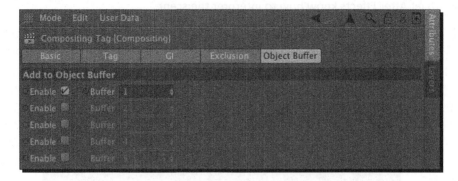

3. Open your **Render Settings** window. Click on the **Multi-Pass** button, then select **Object Buffer**:

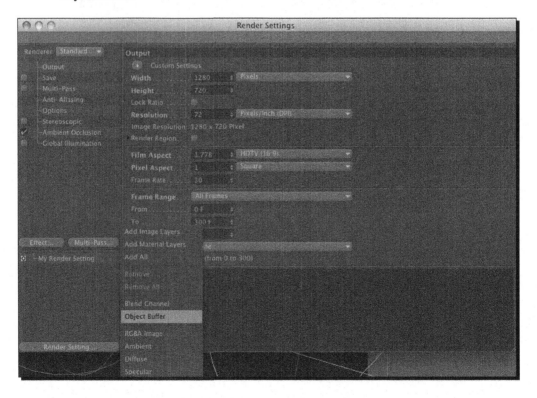

4. The **Object Buffer Pass** should now be added as a child of the **Multi-Pass** setting. The **Group ID** should already be set to **1**. If you used a value other than 1 in step 2, make sure this number matches your object buffer value. Check the checkbox for **Multi-Pass** in the left-hand column:

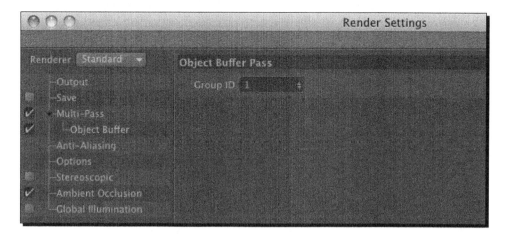

5. Returning to the Objects Manager (we'll be adding another render setting soon, but feel free to close the window for now if it is in your way), make sure the screen object is selected, then navigate to **Tags** | **CINEMA 4D Tags** | **External Compositing**, as shown in the following screenshot:

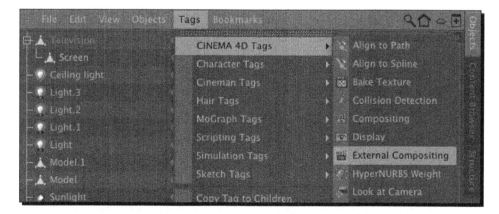

6. With the **External Compositing** tag selected, take a look at the Attributes Manager. Check the **Solid** box. The Object Buffer settings create a null object at the correct position and rotation in 3D space for After Effects, but the **External Compositing** tag will allow us to create a plane at that position with the correct dimensions. Our Coordinates Manager tells us that the plane is **126 x 69**, so let's set the X and Y coordinates accordingly:

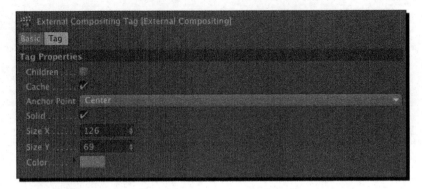

7. In the **Save** tab, expand the window for **Compositing Project File**. Click on the checkbox for **Save**, as well as **Include 3D Data**. We will be exporting to After Effects, but if you click on the drop-down menu, you'll see the other software options available. Then, click on **Save Project File**, and select a location for your new file as shown in the next screenshot. This will create an After Effects Compositing (AEC) file that contains 3D data set up for importing into After Effects. This does not replace your .c4d file; it's important to keep both:

What just happened?

All of the steps we've just taken will be standard for any scene you want to export to After Effects. The basic steps are as follows:

1. Add a compositing tag to the object you'll be using in postproduction.
2. Enable its **Object Buffer**.
3. Add the **Object Buffer** in the **Render Settings** window (make sure their values are identical).
4. Add an **External Compositing** tag to the object.
5. If necessary, turn the object into a solid and specify its dimensions (otherwise, just position data will be preserved).

That's it! Now, we'll look at an additional type of compositing information that can be used in After Effects—**Multi-Pass** rendering.

Render settings for compositing and multipass

So far, we've created a compositing file that will allow us to composite 2D objects into our renders in After Effects. At this point, we'll need to render our scene, but let's set up a couple of extra options first.

As we discussed previously, in addition to compositing in new images and objects in 3D space, we can also allow ourselves much more visual control in post-production by rendering out a series of layered images. These layered images are called passes—shadow passes, luminance passes, and so on. You can add as many different passes as you like; there's no right or wrong answer, it's just dependent on your scene.

The full list of passes is located in your **Render Settings** window. Click on the **Multi-Pass** button to expand the window and take a look at your options:

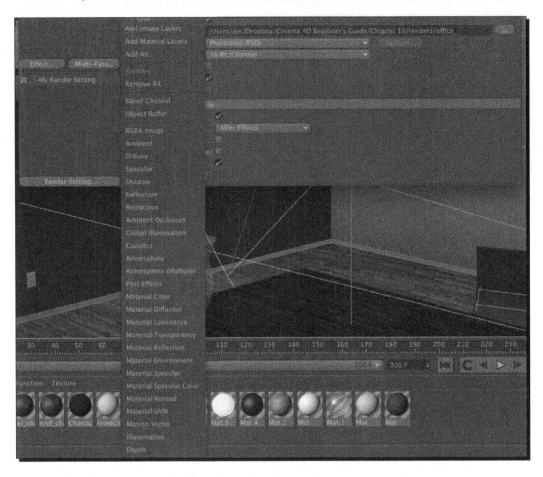

From the list of **Multi-Pass** options, enable **RGBA Image**, **Shadow**, **Ambient Occlusion**, and **Material Luminance**. Feel free to add on any other passes that you'd like to experiment with—this will not increase render time, since Cinema has to calculate the same information no matter what, and it will allow you to see how each of the individual passes work.

Just like the regular image save option, you'll need to enable **Multi-Pass** rendering and give your images a location. Each individual pass will be its own file, so if you render six separate passes for 300 frames, that will result in 1,800 images. You may want to save passes in a different folder:

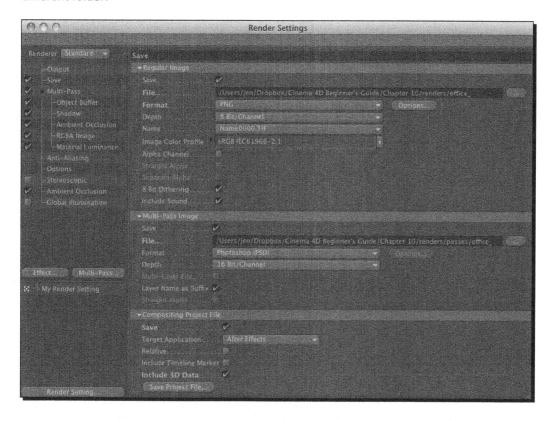

If you are using your original animation with lights turned on, you may want to key your luminance channel on the new television screen material, or turn it off entirely, otherwise the screen will be illuminated at the beginning of your render. This can be controlled in post production, but will be easiest to do before rendering.

As you wait for your file to render, you can take a look at how the individual passes work by opening the **Layer** tab in the **Picture Viewer**. Some of the individual passes will be difficult to understand at the beginning of the animation, since the lights are animating. The next screenshot shows just the Ambient Occlusion pass. The layer is set to **Multiply**, which will be helpful when we import the sequence into After Effects.

Note that if you will be doing compositing that requires an alpha channel, that needs to be specified in your **Render settings** under the **Save** tab. Some image types do not have the ability to preserve alpha channels (such as JPEG), so you will want to select an appropriate format like PNG or TGA. Also make sure that you have the **Alpha Channel** checkbox selected:

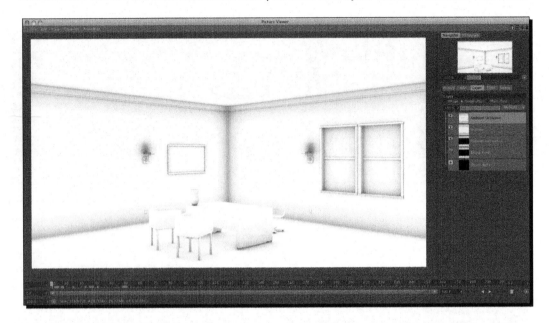

We will be focusing on After Effects for the most part, since we've created an animation, but any of these individual images can be composited in Photoshop as a still image as well.

After you've rendered a couple of frames, take a look at the folder that contains them. You'll notice that each of the passes has a separate extension appended, that is, `office__ao####.psd` for ambient occlusion, `office__matlum####.psd` for material luminance, and so on. This keeps all your passes next to one another in the folder in case you need to import them separately. You can divide them out into individual folders if that makes it easier for you to keep track of them, but by default, After Effects will search for them in their original location:

Next, we'll import the sequence into After Effects. If your images haven't finished rendering, you can still import the sequence early, but you may get warnings about missing frames and will need to reload the footage. If your renders will take some time and you're itching to get started, however, there's no major harm in jumping in early!

Time for action – compositing with Adobe After Effects

Before you get started in After Effects, you will most likely need to install a plugin by performing the following steps:

1. On a PC, this file is named `CINEMA4DAE.aex`; on a Mac it will be called `C4D.plugin`. You can search your hard drive for these files, or navigate to the `Exchange Plugins` folder in the Cinema 4D directory. If for some reason you do not find this file on your hard drive, it can be found on Maxon's website at `http://www.maxon.net/downloads/updates/plugins.html`.

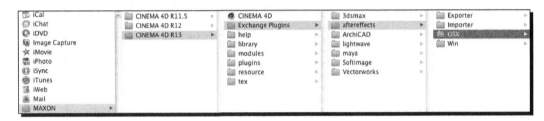

Copy this plugin into the After Effects plugin directory:

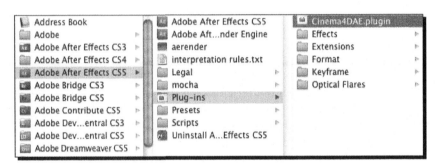

2. Within Cinema, re-save your `.aec` file so that it has the most current information. If you saved your file before adding the multi-pass layers, the `.aec` file will not know to look for them, so there's no harm in updating this file periodically.

3. After you've installed the exchange plugin, open Adobe After Effects. Navigate to **File | Import | File**. Then, select the `.aec` file from your office scene:

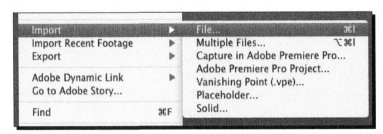

Once you've imported the `.aec` file, save it, then open up the main composition. For simplicity, rearrange your file to look like the following one by moving all passes into the `Special Passes` folder, and deleting the passes currently in the composition. Add in the flat render. If you have multiple cameras, make sure you're looking through whichever camera you used for your render:

As you scroll through your timeline, you'll notice that your lights and the screen object line up perfectly with the camera. Cinema has exported all of its camera data and light information to After Effects, which allows us to add in any 2D data to the scene without requiring a re-render! The possibilities for this feature are endless, from things as simple as adding a video to our television screen to exporting the animation data from a dynamically driven MoGraph scene.

4. To add a video to the television screen, select the **Screen** solid (which should appear as a bright red plane) and pre-compose it (*command* + *Shift* + *C*, or by navigating to **Layer | Pre-compose**). On the pop-up dialog, select the **Leave all attributes in [your comp name]** option, and check the box for **Open New Composition**, then click on **OK**:

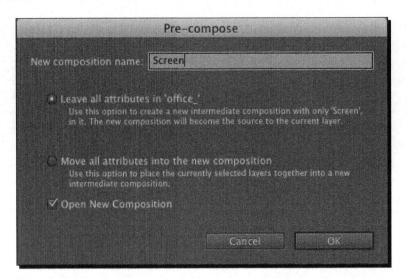

You now have a new, flat composition for the screen. It's currently the exact same size in pixels as it was in centimeters in our Cinema composition. We'll probably want a larger area to work with. Open up the **Composition Settings** (*command* + *K* on your keyboard, or navigate to **Composition | Composition Settings**). Click on the **Lock Aspect Ratio** checkbox. The larger we make this composition, the smaller we'll need to scale it in our full composition, so let's make things easier on ourselves by making it exactly 10 times as large. You can add a zero to either the width or the height, or use Adobe After Effects' built-in math commands and change the **Width** value to `126*10`. Your new dimensions should be **1260** x **690**. Click on **OK** to accept the new settings:

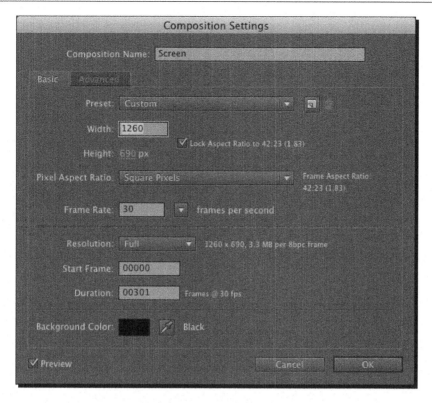

5. Turn off the **Screen** layer's visibility. If you have a Quicktime movie you'd like to use on the screen, you can import it now. The following example will use a sample animation from the Cinema installation, located in the root Cinema 4D installation folder at `CINEMA 4D R13\tex\tutorials\no_keyframes.mov`. If you use a Quicktime movie, make sure to copy it into your project's texture folder. You can also create your own unique animation inside the screen composition.

If you use the `no_keyframes.mov` file, you'll notice that it isn't quite long enough for our composition. You can use the **Time Remap** command to lengthen the footage, but you may find that the animation looks choppy. Instead, let's line the end frame of the animation up with the end frame of our animation, which should make the clip begin around frame **138**:

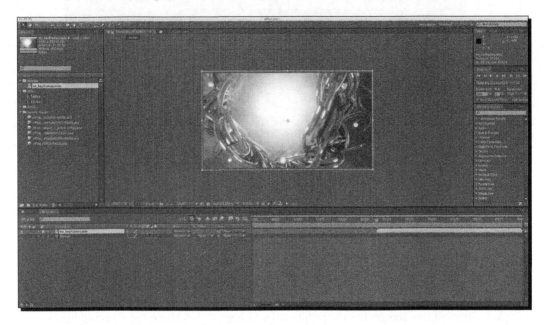

6. Returning to the office scene, you'll notice that our precomp is now far too large for the scene, due to the increase in its size. Change the scale to **10** percent. Then, let's key the opacity from 0-100 percent over 30 frames, beginning at the first frame of the embedded animation (0 percent opacity at frame **138**, 100 percent opacity at frame **168**):

The screen looks a little out of place, though, due to its brightness, and we've lost the ambient occlusion around the edges. Let's make a couple of additional modifications to our screen object.

7. Change the layering mode to **Overlay**. This will make our screen blend a little better with the environment:

8. Open up all keyframes on the object (by using the drop-down menus, or by pressing *U* on your keyboard). You'll notice that there are beginning and ending keyframes for the object, even though it isn't animated. Cinema does this by default to make sure objects stay where they're intended to be, however, in this case we can delete them. Turn off the animation for everything except **Opacity**. This will delete all keyframes, but leave the position and rotation at their correct values:

9. Expand **Material Options**, and you'll notice that **Accepts Lights** is turned on by default. There are many times when this is helpful, however, in this case we should turn it off. Since a television screen gives off light, we don't want there to be any unnecessary hotspots on its surface:

Now our television looks much more appropriate to the scene, and if we need to change anything about its image, we can do it without having to re-render out of Cinema!

10. Imagine that you're unhappy with the Ambient Occlusion settings and wish they were a little darker. Select the **Ambient Occlusion** pass (in the `Special Passes` folder, with `_ao` appended) and drag it on top of your regular render in the composition. Set its mode to **Multiply**, then drag the opacity settings to experiment with the result. You can also do this with the **Shadow Pass**, as well as any other special passes you specified in your render settings (note that certain passes will require different modes):

11. When you're happy with what you've created, export your render out of After Effects with any settings you choose (*command+M* on your keyboard, or by navigating to **Composition | Make Movie**), and you're done!

What just happened?

Using multipass rendering and external compositing data, we've taken a scene out of C4D and into After Effects, where we can composite in additional images and footage without having to fully re-render. As you continue to create motion graphics scenes and your projects become more complex, you are likely to rely on this versatile aspect more and more.

Have a go hero – bringing it all together

We've learned a lot over these ten chapters! It will be rare to ever use all of the skills you've acquired in a single scene, but you now have a wide knowledge base that you can use as you come up with new ideas to create.

As a final exercise, think back on everything you've learned, choose a couple of concepts, and create an animation of your very own that combines them in new, interesting ways. Here are a couple of ideas to get you started:

◆ An outdoor scene with grassy hills created using the Hair module, with an animated sunrise and a car driving through (with wheels linked through XPresso, of course!).

◆ A bag or handkerchief created using the Cloth module, with marbles falling into it from above and colliding with one another using the MoGraph module.

◆ An interior scene that builds itself from nothing, using a combination of MoGraph objects and keyed display tags to make everything appear at just the right time.

◆ Whatever you choose, you've got the skills to bring things together. Plan your project from the beginning, set up objects logically, and the possibilities will be endless.

Summary

Congratulations! You've worked your way through the entire 3D animation process. In the chapters of this book, we've learned how to create models, add texture and lighting, and now we've fully composited our final product.

In this chapter, we covered how to use XRefs to simplify the geometry in our models and cross-reference between files, how to use compositing tags to prepare our files for use in third-party software such as Adobe After Effects, how to create multiple passes to allow for in-depth visual modifications in post production, how to import our compositing data and special passes into After Effects, and how to work with multiple layers and 3D data to create a final product.

The tools we've explored here will give you a solid foundation to keep learning and experimenting with Cinema 4D. Now that you've got multiple animations under your belt, the sky's the limit. Happy rendering!

Pop Quiz Answers

Chapter 2 – Modeling Part 1: Edges, Faces, and Points

Pop quiz – reviewing our toolset

Questions	Answers
Q1. We're working with a complex scene and would like to view an object from our current camera's perspective, but there's another object blocking it in our environment. Without switching cameras, how can we temporarily hide the foreground object?	1 . Double-click the top dot to the right of the object's name in the Object Manager. The dot should be red and this should disable the object's visibility in the viewport (the bottom dot would change its visibility in the renderer).
Q2. We've created an object whose face is subdivided into five sections along the Y axis and need to ensure that the center section is uniformly 15 cm wide. Which tools would we use to select this group of polygons?	2. Navigate to **Select	Loop Selection** while in Polygon Mode and then select the center group of polygons.
Q3. We need to create a basic flagpole with a flat square base and a tall center pole. Which tools would we use to create this model?	3. There are two methods that would be acceptable to create a flagpole. Method one: Create two primitives—a cube for the base and either a second cube or a cylinder for the pole and adjust their proportions accordingly Method two: Create a cube primitive for the base, use Inner Extrude to create a smaller center polygon, and use Extrude to bring it up to the desired height of the flagpole

Chapter 5 – Lighting and Rendering

Pop quiz – lighting and rendering basics

Questions	Answers
Q1. In order to ensure consistency, which render settings should be considered when setting up a scene?	1. Anti aliasing, Global Illumination, and Ambient Occlusion should be considered early in a scene's creation to ensure visual consistency.
Q2. What are the basic types of lights, and how are they created?	2. Omni, Spot, Area, and Infinite. They can be created either through the Lighting menu in the top toolbar or by changing the drop-down menu under the general tab on the light.
Q3. One specific object in a scene appears too blown out, but nearby objects all look as they should. What are two possible solutions?	3. If all objects in the scene appear correct, it may be a problem with the material. If an object is too blown out, perhaps reducing the specular values will help. If it is unnecessary dull, attempt to increase the values. If it's clear that the issue is coming from the placement of a light, consider excluding the object from just that specific light, and if absolutely necessary, create a separate light that only includes the offending object.

Index

Thank you for buying
Cinema 4D Beginner's Guide

About Packt Publishing

Packt, pronounced 'packed', published its first book "Mastering phpMyAdmin for Effective MySQL Management" in April 2004 and subsequently continued to specialize in publishing highly focused books on specific technologies and solutions.

Our books and publications share the experiences of your fellow IT professionals in adapting and customizing today's systems, applications, and frameworks. Our solution-based books give you the knowledge and power to customize the software and technologies you're using to get the job done. Packt books are more specific and less general than the IT books you have seen in the past. Our unique business model allows us to bring you more focused information, giving you more of what you need to know, and less of what you don't.

Packt is a modern, yet unique publishing company, which focuses on producing quality, cutting-edge books for communities of developers, administrators, and newbies alike. For more information, please visit our website: www.PacktPub.com.

Writing for Packt

We welcome all inquiries from people who are interested in authoring. Book proposals should be sent to author@packtpub.com. If your book idea is still at an early stage and you would like to discuss it first before writing a formal book proposal, contact us; one of our commissioning editors will get in touch with you.

We're not just looking for published authors; if you have strong technical skills but no writing experience, our experienced editors can help you develop a writing career, or simply get some additional reward for your expertise.

Unity iOS Game Development Beginners Guide

ISBN: 978-1-84969-040-9   Paperback:314 pages

Develop iOS games from concept to cash flow using Unity

1. Dive straight into game development with no previous Unity or iOS experience

2. Work through the entire lifecycle of developing games for iOS

3. Add multiplayer, input controls, debugging, in app and micro payments to your game

4. Implement the different business models that will enable you to make money on iOS games

Unity 3.x Scripting

ISBN: 978-1-84969-230-4   Paperback: 292 pages

Write efficient, reusable scripts to build custom characters, game environments, and control enemy AI in your Unity game

1. Make your characters interact with buttons and program triggered action sequences

2. Create custom characters and code dynamic objects and players' interaction with them

3. Synchronize movement of character and environmental objects

4. Add and control animations to new and existing characters

Please check **www.PacktPub.com** for information on our titles

Lightning Source UK Ltd.
Milton Keynes UK
UKOW07f0611191116
287977UK00008B/169/P